# PHOTOSHOP FACE TO FACE

GAVIN CROMHOUT
JOSH FALLON
NATHAN FLOOD
KATY FREER
JIM HANNAH
ADRIAN LUNA
DOUGLAS MULLEN
FRANCINE SPIEGEL
JAMES WIDEGREN

friendsof

**Photoshop Face to Face**

© 2002 friends of ED

First printed June 2002

**Trademark Acknowledgements**

friends of ED has endeavored to provide trademark information about all the companies and products mentioned in this book by the appropriate use of capitals. However, friends of ED cannot guarantee the accuracy of this information.

Published by **friends of ED**
30 – 32 Lincoln Road, Olton, Birmingham,
B27 6PA, UK.

Printed in USA.

**ISBN** 1-903450-84-5

**Credits**

**Authors**
Gavin Cromhout
Josh Fallon
Nathan Flood
Katy Freer
Jim Hannah
Adrian Luna
Douglas Mullen
Francine Spiegel
James Widegren

**Commissioning Editor**
James Andrew

**Designer**
Katy Lou

**Editors**
Adam Juniper
James Robinson

**Author Agent**
Mel Jehs

**Project Manager**
Simon Brand

**Technical Reviewers**
Alexandra Blackburn
Dan Caylor
Kim Christensen
Corne van Dooren
Jeroen Meeuwissen
Steph Ridley
Andrew Toumazou

**Indexer**
Simon Collins

**Proofing**
Victoria Blackburn
Pam Brand

**Managing Editor**
Chris Hindley

# CONTENTS

### Gavin Cromhout [Facial Retouching // Sequences]

Gavin Cromhout lives in Cape Town, South Africa and, by a string of coincidences, has done so all his life. He studied both art and psychology at the University of Cape Town, working towards a Masters degree in psychology dealing with facial recognition in Autistic children. You can catch up with him on http://www.lodestone.co.za

### Josh Fallon [Unsettling Portraits]

Josh Fallon resides in Los Angeles, providing illustration and web design services. Fallon's illustration work has been featured by Adobe.com, Computer Arts Special magazine, and in New Masters of Photoshop. Josh lives a double-life as an in-house corporate designer by day and freelance illustrator/web designer by night. He also stays busy working on pet project DesignLaunchpad.com, a resource for beginning graphic designers. Josh's work can be seen at FallonDesign.com. Josh would like to thank the "freaks" that participated in the photo shoot and apologizes in advance to anyone who is frightened by their final photo...

### Nathan Flood [Fantasy]

Nathan Flood is an art director/digital artist living in New York City, NY. He is also the founder and creative partner of NGINCO. He has previously been a creative at WDDG, Vir2L, and Razorfish, and is also a partner/member of THREE.OH. Nathan would like to thank the following artists/composers, without whom, his portraits would not have been possible: Mogwai, Tool, Tricky, Pantera, Philip Glass, The Fantômas, Carl Orff and Leafcutter John.

http://nginco.com
http://threeoh.com
http://wddg.com
http://vir2l.com
http://razorfish.com

### Katy Freer [Art Mimicry]

Katy Freer is centered in Somerset. She likes making things. In the pursuit of making as many new things as possible, Katy has worked with as many media as she has been able to lay her hands on for upwards of two decades. Much love to ma famille et krissy b et la poddington pea.

### Jim Hannah [Art Mimicry]

Jim Hannah has been a sham designer for some time. He kicks lumps out of Photoshop on a regular basis, and has also squeezed money out of magazine owners by carving up their pages with PageMaker. Imagine! Not even Quark! The only person who's ever seen through this façade is his art teacher, Mrs Cannell, who cried Laziness, and who'll just be seething that he managed to slouch into a publication – and a color one, too! Kudos to Jols for the understanding.

## Adrian Luna [Contexts]

Adrian has been searching for his edge for many years, and has endeavored upon many creative theories and methods that have become a base formula for his designs. Everyday is a new canvas for learning and time is simply an open window for opportunity.

By day he is a graphic designer working with clients on projects ranging from Flash animation engines, online or offline interactive systems, entertainment websites, delicate print materials, and creative high-res imagery. By night he is a new media artist working hard to create inspirational material as a video artist, author, photographer, and creative visionary. Adrian has seven years' user interface experience with such clients as Adidas, Sempra Energy, Home Depot, Farmers Insurance, Beckton Dickinson, Duke University Medical Center, and William Morris Agency. He is currently expanding his client base with http://www.the-belly.com/ working with such clients as USA Films with Robert Altman, Universal Interactive with Nintendo, Ezekiel Clothing, and Hotkiss Fashion.

His true love after good Graphic Design, New Media, and Modern Architecture is his family. Adrian is celebrating the new welcome of his precious 2 year-old son Derek and is enjoying every moment of their daily life together. He would like to dedicate his chapter to his lovely wife, Amber.

## Douglas Mullen [From Scratch]

Douglas Mullen lives and works in Scotland. He studied illustration, design and photography at Duncan of Jordanstone College of Art & Design, where he subsequently returned to study theory in the Master of Design program. He works mainly freelance, and also as a part-time lecturer in graphic design, illustration and digital media. He has won numerous awards and commendations over the past few years for exhibition and multimedia work. Douglas works under the name 'd-10' which brings together illustration, graphic design and photography into one complete environment. d-10 itself consists of commercial work and personal ideas. www.d-10.net

## Francine Spiegel [Color Creativity]

Francine Spiegel is originally from Miami Beach, Florida. After graduating in painting from Rhode Island School of Design in 1997, she moved to Brooklyn and is now on her way to Los Angeles, California. The past few years she has concentrated primarily on airbrush painting, digital work for print, and animation. Francine's work has been published in Vice and Spin Magazine and her personal work can be seen on tenderoni.com. She is currently getting back into drawing with a ballpoint pen and is participating in a new milkyelephant.com CD-ROM with artists that inspire her very much.

## James Widegren [Fantasy]

Acclaimed Swedish designer James Widegren studied Media Communication before co-founding the company Nisch Interactive. He is the driving force behind the design site threeoh.com, a forum for the promotion of well-designed communications media, and a vital resource for the online design community – not to mention the May 1st Reboot event that orchestrated ca 1700 websites around the globe in a show of unified collaboration. It was the first and largest international mass launch in Internet history.

James began his career with Razorfish and Vir2L before taking up his current role as freelance Art Director for several high-profile clients such as General Motors, Sony and CBS Sports. He is Chief Creative Officer of threeoh.com and is recognized as one of new media's freshest talents. He continually wins accolades for various design projects, and has an impressive list of publications under his belt. While serving as a Sr. Art Director at Vir2L, James contributed to the Vir2L Forum site which won the New York Festivals New Media Competition, Cannes Cyber Lion: Gold, The Clio Award, Art Directors Club Award, and The Invision Award.

Personal
www.idiocase.com   www.threeoh.com   www.threeoh.com/may1/   www.may1reboot.com

Related
www.nisch.com   www.razorfish.com   www.vir2l.com

**A word about versioning**

This book is aimed at Photoshop 6 and 7. Our first chapter offers a tantalizing look at the future of Photoshop, examining the new image manipulation features on offer in Photoshop 7. Never before has it been so easy to make sophisticated changes to an image, whether it's reality or creativity you're after.

However, every other project in the book is compatible with Photoshop 6, and, to a large extent, versions as early as 5. Our authors variously use PCs and Macs, so we have kept screenshots in alignment with the system they used. In the text, we have made sure that both Mac and PC commands have been supplied.

**Downloads and Support**

If you would like to produce the results as shown in the book, you'll need to download the original image files. These can be found at www.friendsofed.com/facetoface.

If you have any comments, please contact us – we'd love to hear from you! If you visit our web site at www.friendsofed.com, you will find a range of contact details, or you can use feedback@friendsofed.com. The editors and authors will deal with any difficulties you may have quickly and efficiently.

There's a host of other features on the site that may interest you; interviews with top designers, samples from our other books, and a message board where you can post you questions, discussions, and answers.

**Preface** *[Pre-face]*

A leading Photoshop professional recently said to us that no-one, not even he, could know all there is to know about Photoshop. It's just too various, too broad, too sensitive to be able to absorb it in full. There is *always* another trick to learn. *Always* another method. The real talent is in approaching it in a way that appeals to you, and then taking it on yourself and pushing it as far as you can.

The idea behind this book is to offer you a series of strictly limited canvases, which have been taken by some of the finest designers around and pushed into new realms. The limits we chose were those of everyone's favorite image: the face.

The resulting collection of work is an explosion of ideas, technique and interpretation. In these few chapters we have the broadest imaginable cross-section of styles. We have photorealistic techniques. We have face painting, oil painting, screen-printing, and mixed media. We dabble with hyper-reality, surreality, fantasy, romance, New Romance, horror, tension and serenity. From a collection of everyday faces, we have generated a cast of entirely digital characters – clowns, tigers, glamour pusses, angels, demons, rock stars, monsters, and ghosts.

With suggestions and tips coming from the authors, together with many in-depth tutorials, you will come away from this book bursting with ideas, and equipped with the knowledge of how to coax the subtlest expression out of Photoshop.

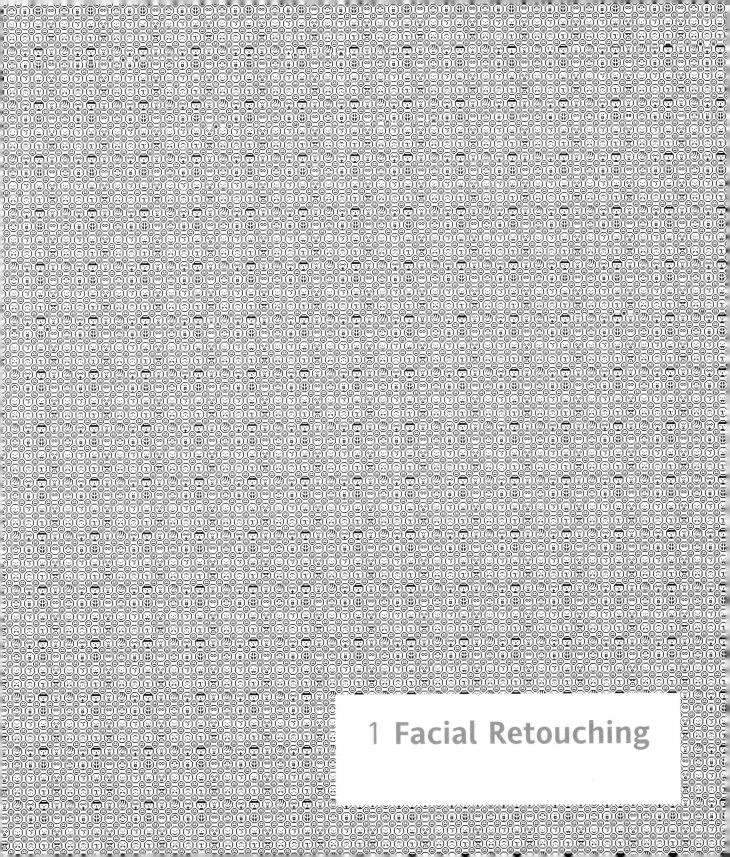

1 **Facial Retouching**

Faces are strange things. How is it possible that you can recognize someone you haven't seen in twenty years? Their hair is a different color and almost certainly a different length, and their skin is less elastic – giving a different morphology to the face. Along with this change would be the presence of wrinkles; perhaps the eyes would still be the same, but even eyes change color with time. It's possible, though, to catch a glimpse of someone in a crowd, in poor lighting, out of their usual context, or even just catch a glimpse of their side profile, but you're still able to recognize them. Strange, but often true. Try this out at a high-school reunion...

It seems that knowing faces is a built-in trait – some studies have shown that newly born babies orient towards white boards with three black blobs on (to represent the eyes and mouth) significantly more than any other arrangement. We know and can interpret faces perhaps at a finer level than any other changing shape. Working with faces in Photoshop is therefore perhaps one of the most interesting, and in turn, difficult things to do. I say 'difficult', because to change someone's face in a believable way often requires being immensely subtle.

In this chapter, and those to follow, we will look at some of the ways faces can be retouched, using the enhanced tools of Adobe's new version, Photoshop 7.

By way of addressing these three topics we will look at a number of different projects.

## Retouching

In this section, we'll look at basic approaches you may want to adopt when preparing your photos for whatever you may have intended for them. Such approaches lay the foundation for the more fundamental or radical changes and enhancements that you're likely to make later on. You'll find it's worthwhile to invest time touching up images before progressing any further.

### Clearing the complexion

Before you can even start adding special effects to your images, there are often a number of hurdles to overcome. For instance, the effect of an ethereal looking face is pretty much ruined by a large pimple...if only it wasn't there! Removing most of these tiny blemishes is a fairly easy task with Photoshop, as we'll soon see.

Sometimes, it's not even a blemish that's the problem; it might be something as simple as a discoloration of the skin. In any event, Photoshop has a number of tools created for the specific task of removing small, unwanted areas from an image – especially useful when we come to dealing with faces, as no face is perfect.

Have a look at the following image:

In this image the lighting and composition are fairly good. There are a number of niggling small problems that can easily be removed. Before we begin, an important, if not the most important point, to consider:

Everyone is an expert on faces. Any changes you make, if you want them to be believable, will have to be subtle and natural.

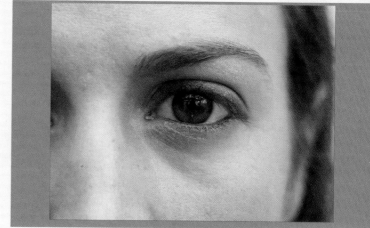

The first thing we need to do is make a list of the problems and decide on an order to tackle them:

1. There are a few tiny spots around the nose.

2. There are some burst blood vessels in the cheeks.

3. There is a tiny scar on the bridge of the nose.

4. There is a slight yellowing just to the left of the iris.

We'll start with the easiest problem first – getting rid of a few spots here and there. Before we start, though, it's worth mentioning that it's good practice to always duplicate your background layer. I'm always paranoid that I'm going to irreparably alter the original and therefore have no point of reference, so I always make a copy, just in case.

## Stamping out spots

The image below identifies the spots that we need to tend to, so let's get onto it...

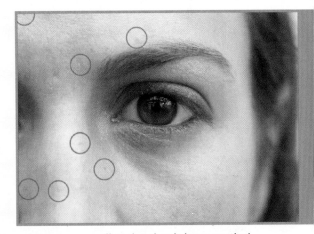

Photoshop 7 – like previous versions – includes the really ingenious Clone Stamp tool. Basically, it works by allowing the user to select (by ALT-clicking) an area of skin close to the blemish that is untarnished, and then uses that selection as the paint to cover the blemish.

So, instead of using paint, we are using another part of the image. We could have simply selected a color that's very close in hue to an untarnished area near the blemish and used that, but then we'd be creating a spot of flat color, which would basically act as a new blemish. The Clone Stamp tool allows us to preserve the texture while changing the hues of the original image.

With the spot that's positioned to the bottom left of the eye, on the bridge of the nose, you'll notice that it has a vertical gradient of light to dark from left to right, caused by the way the light catches it. If we select an area to paste from (using ALT-click) immediately above the damaged area and then paint on the blemish below, the skin tone and light gradient will be preserved. No amount of painting over this area with a single color could accomplish this task.

The mechanics of using this tool are fairly rudimentary, but to get the most out of it, it's worth considering a number of points:

1. The area that you're getting your raw material from will never be identical to the area you're trying to fix – this is a human face after all. So, if you want to be really subtle, use a low opacity brush (at around 25%) and dab gently over the damaged area – as opposed to using a 100% opacity brush and completing the task with one stroke.

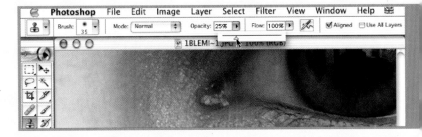

   If you simply paste from one area to the other, you'll get two identical areas appearing right next to each other and form a kind of mini-pattern that's recognizably fake. If you spot any patterns in facial images, the likelihood is that it's been doctored (albeit badly).

2. Use a soft edged Brush – so that the edges of the paste aren't visible.

Right, that takes care of the spots, but what about the scar?

## Healing a scar on the nose

This is a slightly larger area than any one spot. Pasting from any one area will surely create a fairly obvious and recognizable pattern.

The great part about using the Clone Stamp tool is that we're not restricted to using the original unblemished area; we can resample new areas as often as we like. To fix the top of the scar, we can sample an untarnished area from immediately *above* it (which would be most similar in terms of hue, tone and texture). To fix the bottom of the scar we could select a new area to sample from, such as the area just *below* the scar.

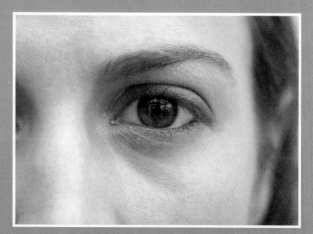

In fact, to remove this scar effectively, we'll sample from all around it, building up the new area from more healthy looking adjacent areas. We can use the same process on the burst blood vessels.

Remember, we are trying to be realistic here, so don't remove every single tiny mark, or you run the risk of losing realism in your final product. It's really important that the texture of your image is preserved when using the Clone Stamp tool, especially with faces. It's pointless if you've got the hue and tonality of the area right, but suddenly the pores of the skin end in a suspiciously smooth area.

You can see in the top image that this exact problem has occurred and there's a suspiciously smooth area around the bridge of the nose, where we removed the scar.

It would be great if we could use some of the texture from the forehead to paste over this area, but if we used the Clone Stamp tool to select some of the forehead and then pasted it over the affected area, the tonality would be completely wrong. The forehead is far lighter, so our change would look unnatural and really stand out.

Enter the Healing Brush tool – new to Photoshop 7.

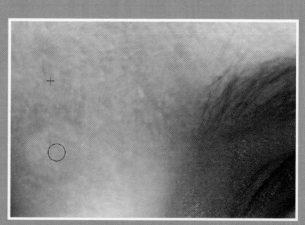

 The Healing Brush tool works in much the same way as the Clone Stamp tool, except that once you let go of the mouse, it automatically matches the tone of the area you're pasting to. This means that when we borrow from the forehead area and paste it over the smooth scar area, it makes the borrowed material appropriately darker so that it blends in correctly. You'll find the difference to be subtle, but if you want to achieve realism, it's very effective.

## Retouching the eye

Our final task on this project is getting rid of the yellow area of the eye. We have a different problem here – the tone and texture of the area are correct; it's just the hue that's gone awry.

This is a slightly longer procedure than spot removal. Obviously, there are lots of different ways to achieve this task. I chose the approach that we'll be using for two reasons:

- It preserves the underlying textures of the eye, so it looks more real.

■ It can be altered at any time. If you're working on multiple aspects of an image, it's useful to be able to come back and change something at a later date without having to redo all the tasks involved.

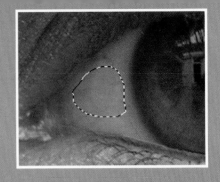

Using the same proximity you would with the Clone Stamp tool, choose a color immediately adjacent to the damaged area and make this your foreground color. In this case, it's a light reddish gray color. Now we need to marquee the damaged area using the Lasso tool.

It's now time to add a Hue/Saturation adjustment layer. As we have an existing marquee, the adjustment layer will only be applied to that area.

Remember to check the Colorize option, which will take all the colors in our selected area (within the marquee) and replace the hues using the foreground color whilst keeping the tonality intact. This basically means that the damaged area of the eye is recolored using only our foreground color – which we chose from an undamaged part of the eye. So, whilst the color changes, the texture (tonality) remains the same.

All that remains to be done is to blur the edges of the adjustment layer mask where our marquee (affected area) ends, so that the change from the adjustment colors to the unretouched eye is less abrupt. This means working on the mask layer with a soft edged black brush at low opacity. Going around the edges of the affected area with this will gradually remove the effect, thus blending everything more seamlessly. There are also a few light speckles just to the right of the discolored area, which the Clone Stamp tool can take care of. Finally, I removed the visible blood vessel just above this area.

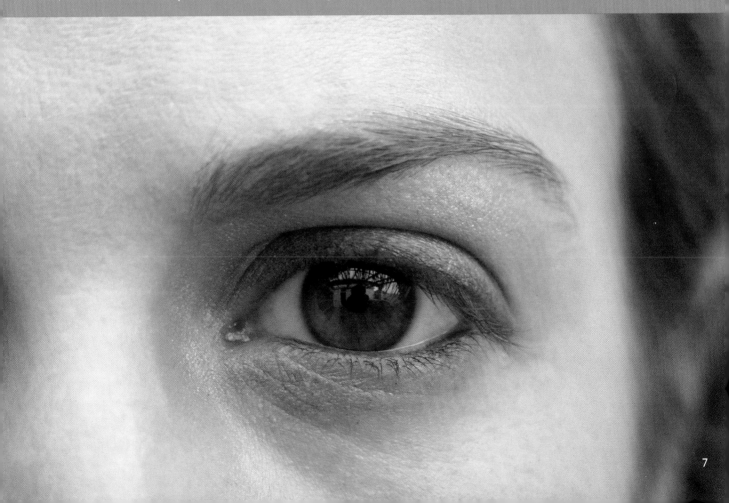

## Poor photography

Not every photograph can be taken perfectly. I recall several thousand photographs that I've taken that have fallen into this less than perfect category.

A classic problem, is experiencing red eye. This is far less contagious than pink eye, and a lot easier to clear up. Red eye happens when the flash you're using ricochets off the back of the wall of the eye and reflects back out into the shot. Some of the more modern cameras have anti-red eye measures – like creating a pre-flash to constrict the pupil, meaning less light can enter and escape from it.

Regardless of this, it's still perfectly easy to have red eye creeping into your shots. In fact, I'm particularly good at it!

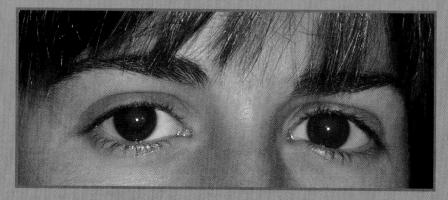

Getting rid of red eye is about as easy as getting it in the first place. There are two main ways to tackle the problem:

First, select the offending area using the Elliptical Marquee tool. Remember that if you start your ellipse – don't let go of the mouse pointer, and hold Spacebar briefly to move the whole shape. Now create a new layer and fill the selected area with black. Now if we change the blending mode to Overlay, we're almost there already:

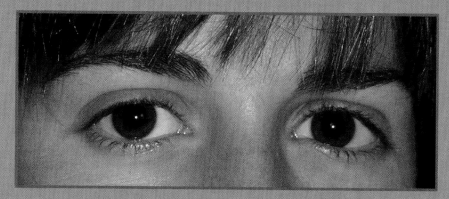

The glint in the eye is still red, though. To fix this we are once again going to select the pupil area, but this time introduce a Hue/Saturation adjustment layer. All that we need to do is drop the saturation down all the way to −100 and there's no more red eye.

The other method of removing red eye involves using the Replace Color command. Basically, you select all the red hues using **Select > Color Range...** then click on the red areas of the eye. The areas that will be selected show up in the preview as white on black – you can then adjust them by reducing their saturation and brightness.

While this is often fairly successful, I find that it isn't as useful as the first technique for two reasons.

- The darker tones of the red eye and the brown of the iris have similar tones, making it difficult to isolate just the red colors that you want.

- The controls available for altering the chosen colors (presuming you manage to do this) are very limited; only saturation and brightness will be of use. Using the brightness command like this will remove a fair amount of the highlights in the eye, such as the tiny spots of reflection, thus reducing realism.

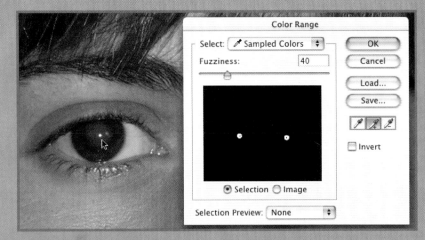

In any event, using the former technique is faster, and gives us an acceptable result, as you can see below:

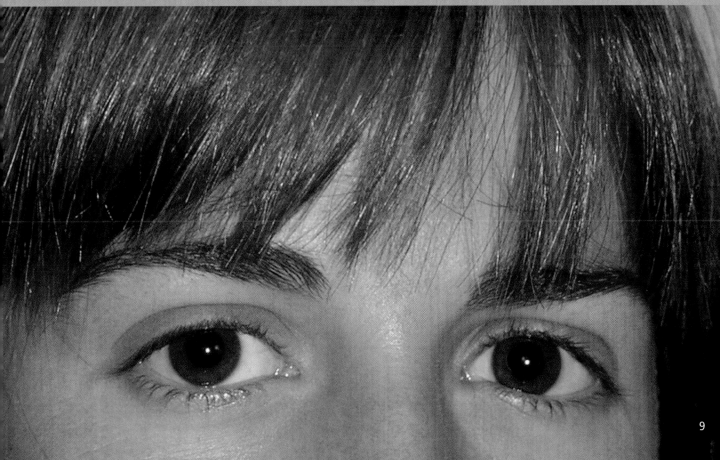

## Adding special lighting effects

Correcting an image is normally just the first step in working with faces. Often we will want to enhance the photograph to improve the overall impact. An important technique in this regard deals with improving the way the image is lit. Even with good lighting on a face, the overall effect can sometimes look quite flat.

Faces have the most amazing number of curves (try modeling one in 3D if you don't believe me), and it's often nice to accentuate facial curves. Part of the beauty of a face is the play of light along it, so a good way to start enhancing a facial image is by enhancing or reintroducing the face's tonal flow.

One of the most difficult types of faces to work with is the bearded one. Beards break up the play of light across the face, but let's see what we can do to fix this.

This picture was taken in fairly harsh light and as a result, the tone and color of the image has been negatively affected.

As we change the lighting of the image, its color will be affected, meaning we'll have to tweak it a little. The original color of the image isn't great to start with, but we're going to make it far worse. If we stopped and analyzed what needed to be done on the image before starting to alter it, we would probably concentrate on two areas: Fixing the lighting and fixing the color.

The reason that I've chosen to fix the lighting first is because doing so will affect the color. If we started by fixing the color and then went on to fix the lighting, this would to some extent mess up the color changes previously made.

We start by duplicating the background layer twice and then changing the blending mode to Color Burn – I'm trying to bring out the light to create some contrast in the overall lighting of the face. Next, I'm going to subtly blend this over the original face to enhance the lighting.

I now want to use this Color Burn layer to utilize the fact that it has exaggerated contrast between light and dark areas. However, if I were to use the color burn as is, it would only target very specific areas of the image. Remember, this blending mode works a little bit like increasing the contrast of the image, and the areas that would be most affected would be those at the edges of the tone range – extremely light and dark colors, which would then start to look a little artificial. I'm aiming for a kind of rosy glow to the image, so we need to spread this contrast around a little bit.

I then created a new layer of the entire image so far using the **Select > All** and **Edit >Copy Merged** menu options, and then added a fairly strong Gaussian Blur to help spread the effect.

Now, when I change this layer's blending mode to Screen, a fairly rich glow is added to the image. It proved to be a little too rich for me, so I dropped the opacity of the layer to 80%.

As you can see, the color of the image has been fairly drastically affected because a lot of unwanted red and yellow has crept in from the color burn. So, it's time to normalize the color, which I achieved by adding a solid color adjustment layer using a fairly earthy brown as the fill color, and changing the blending mode to Hue. On the mask of this layer, I used black to remove the effect from the eyes. Not bad, but I think you'll agree that the image now looks a little plastic:

To overcome this, I added a Hue/Saturation adjustment layer and shifted the entire hue range slightly into the red by moving the Hue Slider to -4: enough to reintroduce a realistic looking skin color.

Admittedly, we've lost a fair amount of the color range, which we consciously narrowed by using the Hue blending mode. The Hue/Saturation adjustment layer has not in fact addressed this problem – while we have shifted all the colors, we have not introduced any new ones. To address this I dropped the opacity of the solid color adjustment layer to 80%, which let in a small percentage of the original color.

The end result therefore (hopefully) has the correct blend between interesting tone and aesthetically pleasing color, without departing too radically from being realistic.

So, even though we are dealing with a bearded face, we are still able to introduce an interesting flow of light that enhances the image and increases the visual depth.

## Recoloring

Sometimes we need to adjust the color of an image *before* we start altering the lighting. In the case of this image, fixing the color is far more important than introducing enhancing light elements.

The important thing to look out for when radically changing the color of an image is the way the range of hues is affected – like we encountered with the previous image (even when the amount of change was fairly small).

Poor lighting in this photograph has severely affected the color, giving it an unnatural yellow sheen, so let's see what we can do to change this. In this exercise we're going to apply a lot of adjustment layers, hence preserving the original background layer. We discussed the importance of being able to come back and make changes at a later date earlier in this chapter – we're staying true to this form here.

Now let's add a Hue/Saturation adjustment layer. I just wanted to start chipping away at the skewed color in the image, and at least get the range of color more towards pink than yellow. Similar to our experience with the bearded man, I adjusted the Hue Slider to –4, except this time I also dropped the Saturation Slider down to –27. I also figured that the color present in the image was too rich, so desaturated the image slightly at the same time.

A good start, but the image is way too dark. We need to address this before we can continue altering the image's color.

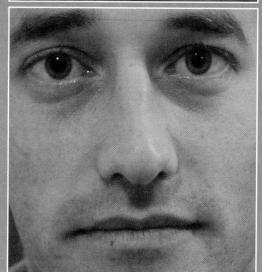

Enter the Brightness/Contrast adjustment layer. In this case I increased both the brightness and the contrast to simply amplify the entire range of color. How much you choose to do this is entirely up to you, depending on your preference and the image you're working on – I used a Brightness value of +35 and Contrast value of +23. At this point, I could have started messing with levels and suchlike, but I knew I still had a fair amount of color manipulation to go before that, so in the meantime (as mentioned), I just raised the entire hue range.

One important thing that I noticed from this was that even though I had drastically changed the brightness of the entire image, the color of the eyes remained fairly dull.

To remedy this, I created another Brightness/Contrast adjustment layer – this time using the mask to isolate the effect to just the eyes (specifically the white areas). On this masked adjustment layer, Brightness is +68 and Contrast is +23.

We're still quite a way from completing the transformation – the face is still lacking in the color and lighting departments. So, making the eyes perfectly white now would mean that they would become overly bright as we addressed different parts of the face. All we're doing now is just subtly making them stand out a bit. If you're working on separate features, it's important to try and maintain an overall, cohesive effect. Artificially enhancing a particular feature so that it stands out from the rest is the wrong approach if you want to maintain realism. The opacity of the layer (and therefore the effectiveness of the effect) was set at around 15%.

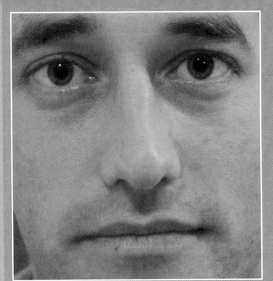

It's definitely looking more real now. I added another Hue/Saturation layer – this time desaturating a little more, and increasing the brightness slightly. This brought the range of color fairly close to normal by introducing some realistic color. Obviously, this is open to interpretation – perhaps I should rather say we're going for *believable* color.

With the addition of this adjustment layer, I felt that the range and tone of color in the image was almost there. Most of the yellow had gone, and even though the image was still a little bit on the dark side, things had certainly progressed. I did, however, feel that the Brightness/Contrast layer had desaturated the overall color of the image a little too much, so I dropped the opacity of the layer down to 60%. This gave me enough of an alteration in the brightness, without the undesirable problems caused by desaturation.

We're almost there – a final Levels adjustment layer should see us through. The most important thing for me at this point was getting enough highlights in the image – I didn't want to have to go and change the brightness of the image again because this would affect the established color range too much.

To achieve this, I altered the whitepoint of the image. That's the great part about the Levels adjustment layer option – we can affect different areas of the image's tone individually – like highlights, midtones and shadows. We can also decide which channel (red, green or blue) gets affected if we feel like tampering with color ranges individually. By adjusting the whitepoint, we are basically picking a color in the image and saying that this is to be the brightest color. We will therefore adjust the brightness of all other colors based on this.

So, if we picked a really dark color, Photoshop would make this color white and adjust all tones accordingly – all tones that are lighter than this (originally dark) color would be made even lighter. Therefore, if we pick a color that's one of the lightest colors in the image, we can basically just pick up all the color and make it lighter. However, unlike using the Brightness/Contrast adjustment layer option, this doesn't wash out the contrast as much.

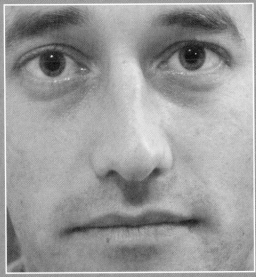

As I stated before, when you're trying to make something realistic, this is an entirely subjective goal. We have, however, managed to effectively increase the color range of the image, and introduce a healthy amount of contrast at the same time.

To complete the color task we added a lot of different adjustment layers, each one slightly changing the image. But how do you know which layers to add when?

While there's no hard and fast rule here, a good point to remember is that when you're trying to alter the color or lighting of an image, realize that it's unlikely you're going to pull it off in one step. As you change the hue, this will often affect the lighting, and visceversa. Start with whatever seems to be the biggest problem. I usually start with the lighting because as we've seen before, if you start by altering the color, a lot of the time you'll have to come back and redo it.

Always be cautious of decreasing the color depth too drastically: Adding a very strong contrast adjustment might remove too much of the image's midtones, which might not be recoverable. Makeup is like Photoshop you can wear: If you plaster too much on too quickly, people can spot it a mile away, so it's worth avoiding!

### Transforming – morphology changes

While a nice diffuse lighting effect (or lengthy session with the Healing Brush tool) can go a long way to removing freckles and even hiding wrinkles, certain structural elements of the face – like the morphology itself, will be relatively unaffected by these alterations.

So how far can we go? Well, with Photoshop the sky is pretty much the limit. In fact – the only real limit is your imagination, and time you have available. Let's look at a combination of all the techniques discussed in this chapter and demonstrate their application in a complete image makeover project. This will help affirm the order of techniques and how the image is likely to progress – from stock standard shot, to finished product.

Let's have a critical look at the image we are going to be working with:

There are a number of areas that we can improve on in this image. Here are the tasks for retouching the face:

- There are some minor skin blemishes to remove.

- Nadia's face is slightly distorted in shape because of the angle she is lying at. We need to rectify this.

- The lighting on her nose is particularly unflattering, making it look bigger than it should. We will need to change either the lighting, or the shape of the nose.

- The shadow on her eyes makes them look rather small; it would be better if they were slightly bigger.

- While the smile dimples are attractive on the left of the face, they make the face look bumpy on the right-hand side, so we'll need to remove them and smooth out the shape of the face.

That about covers the work we need to do on the face. Obviously, different people will find different tasks to address. Altering the look of a face to make it 'more pleasing' is almost entirely subjective. Although there are some aspects of beauty in a face that are universal, such as regularity of features, good skin tone and color, and lack of blemishes – on the whole, you'll have to decide for yourself.

Once we have accomplished these tasks we can address the fairly poor color and lighting in the image.

We've already covered how to get rid of minor blemishes. I had no texture to worry about in this image, so the task was relatively easy, but how do we go about changing the shape of the face?

I accomplished the change in two steps. First, I used the Liquify tool (**Filter > Liquify...**) to smooth out the contour of the face. I used the Warp tool with a brush size of 64 and a pressure of 50. This Warp tool is useful here because it allows you to warp areas of the image independently of each other – like flattening out folds in a napkin. We can therefore subtly change the contour of Nadia's face, without being too obvious.

Changing the entire shape of the face was slightly trickier. Regardless of the shape of the marquee you draw, Photoshop will apply changes to it using a rectangular bounding box. For instance, if you're using a diamond shaped marquee, Photoshop will draw a square around it and resize it according to that square. So the problem is: What if you want to push the sides of the diamond closer together, and not the points?

In the context of the image we have here – if I apply a rectangular marquee around the face and then resize it, the face will be squashed out of proportion – the correctly positioned marquee would be tilted slightly clockwise. What we want to achieve is to narrow the face. I don't like using the distort setting for transforming images, so I rotated the entire image until the face was parallel with the canvas, and then scaled it to narrow the face. The best way to do this would be to use the Measure tool: By drawing a measurement line from eye to eye, Photoshop will tell you the rotation of the line you've just drawn, from 90 degrees. You can then use this angle to counter-rotate the canvas until the line is parallel to the canvas's bottom – also therefore lining the eyes up parallel with the canvas. Once I had done this, I simply rotated it back.

I still found the shape of the face a little too oval. I also wanted to address the issue of the shadow on the eyes, which was making them appear too small. Back to the Liquify tool – I used the Bloat tool on the eyes just to swell their size very slightly and the Warp tool on the contour of the cheek again:

While I was at it, I changed the contour of the nose very slightly, using a smaller (about 35 pixels) brush so I could target just the bridge area. I think I might have got slightly carried away on the shape of the face – it's a lot thinner than the original, but it's amazing to see how much we can actually get away with here!

The color in the image up until now is fairly drab and uninteresting. I decided to change this by going for a healthy summer glow, so the first place to start was with a Color Balance adjustment layer. I tweaked the reds and yellows slightly by shifting the Shadow, Midtone and Highlight Sliders about 4 points towards red, and also towards yellow. This helped to remove a lot of the blue tinge from the original image:

This goes a long way to sorting out the color, but the lighting is still pretty boring. Let's create a glow, similar to the one we completed earlier in the chapter. Once again this involved creating a Merged Layer (**Edit > Copy Merged**), and then using the Color Burn blending mode, which in this example actually gives us quite a nice looking image:

This image brings out the lighting in a far more interesting way. Once again, I applied a Gaussian Blur to the image then created a merged copy of the layer.

When I used Screen as the blending mode for this new layer, the lighting created a healthy looking glow:

This was a little bit too intense and looks a touch unrealistic, so I dropped the opacity of this layer down to 87%. As we've seen before, often the effect you create will push things in the right direction, but will come across a little too forcefully, so for the sake of realism, it's necessary to reduce the effect slightly. Additionally, I masked out the effect on the pillow area in the top left as it was washing the image out too much at that particular point.

My only concern was that the screen had made the image a little bit too yellow, so I introduced a Hue/Saturation adjustment layer, and pulled the image a little bit back towards red – adjusting the sliders about 4 points towards red, and blue for the Shadows, Midtones and Highlights. As you can see, this adjustment is integral in the final result:

## Summary

To summarize, I guess I'm forced to offer some slightly schizophrenic advice. While it's important to plan ahead – and decide in advance what needs to be altered/improved in an image, nothing is quite as powerful as experimentation. Exploring the use of different blending modes for layers is always really interesting when working with faces.

One of the strangest things for me as a young child was to hold up photographic negatives to the light. Here were shapes that I understood, but in totally unnatural colors. Experimenting with different blending modes works along the same lines. If you're just starting out in Photoshop, using faces is a nice way to get into working out how blending modes work – you already understand how a face should look, and it's therefore relatively easy to see how changing the blending modes affect the overall look. If we were working on cars, and we decided to completely change the color range, it might not be so startling. However, change a face to bright blue and you know just what the effect is doing to the original!

In any event, regardless of your skill level with Photoshop, a really valuable exercise is this:

Duplicate an image onto a new layer and apply a blending effect upon it. Make a new layer that is a merged copy of the previous two layers and experiment with altering the blending mode for *this* new layer. We used such a technique in this chapter to create a warm glow in some of the images, but there are lots of different permutations of blending modes to be discovered. Give it a try.

## 2 Unsettling Portraits

Imagine waking on a typical morning and after customarily hitting the snooze button on your alarm clock seven times, you drag yourself into the bathroom. After running cold water through your clammy hands and splashing your face to remove the sleep-generated crust in your eyes, you raise your head to confront your mirror image. How would you react if you discovered that your eyes were solid black? What if one of your eyeballs was missing or if your eyelashes had grown to four times their normal length?

Most people envision these situations and shudder. The graphic artist, however, grins slightly and thinks, "Yeah, that would be sweet to try and pull off in Photoshop!" That's what we're going to attempt in this chapter – take a group of otherwise normal-looking folks (you know the sort of person – one mouth, one nose, two eyes, two ears) and create unsettling portraits. The key here though, is that the intended freakiness will be accomplished through somewhat subtle changes to common facial elements.

When I was envisioning the finished portraits, I was most concerned with making them look as realistic as possible without looking like an obvious computer-generated effect. The prominent danger when adding minor tweaks to a simple photograph like a portrait is that the effects will not mesh with the rest of the image. The aspect of working with digital photography that is usually taken for granted is the fact that with most consumer-level cameras, a certain amount of grain from JPEG artifacts or other types of compression are usually present in an image. While this is fine in itself, it is often a large factor in why smooth computer-generated airbrushing doesn't always blend well in digital photos.

Relying heavily on airbrushing to add effects often creates elements that look way too smooth for the rest of the image. You run into this a lot in portrait retouching – for example, the solid color of an airbrush stroke doesn't always blend well with the varying tones of skin, or hair. Normally, the solution is the Clone Stamp tool, but with these portraits I had to create a lot of elements from scratch. I used certain aspects of the original images as clues to how to perform the modifications and keep them true to reality. I took careful notice of the way the lighting and shadowing in the portraits behaved, and tried to mimic its appearance in the elements that I added or modified. It was usually these small but significant touches that really finished off each piece and gave it an extra touch of realism.

My ultimate aim was to create a collection of portraits that if you quickly flipped through you might not even stop and look twice. At second glance, however, you should notice disturbing or sometimes even comic (wait until you see Jake!) details. So, enjoy my gallery – they'll hopefully still want to talk to me after they've seen what I've done with their faces!

This is my dad Charlie – his portrait was a prime candidate for this effect because I know most people are drawn to his trademark lazy right eyelid. So, I thought that it would be interesting to see what garners initial attention – a lazy eye or one that's missing altogether.

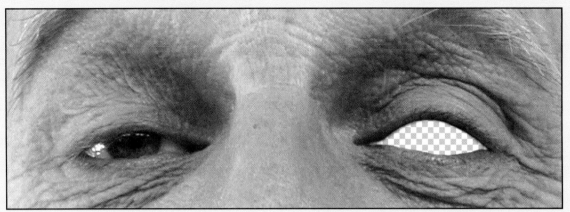

To get started with this image, I first had to clear out the area where the eyeball would become the eye socket. Since I effectively wanted to work behind the shape of the eyelid, the best option here was to mask out the eyeball. To create the mask I simply clicked the mask icon on the layers palette, first making sure I was working on the correct layer. I then used the Airbrush with black paint (black erases, white fills in) to brush out the eye.

If this is unclear, try to imagine it physically – like the skin around a real eye socket; the skin only allows a portion of the eye to be visible, and no matter where the eyeball moves the same area is always masked. So, I used a mask on the only layer of the image so far and used the Airbrush option in the Brushes palette (simply the Airbrush tool in Photoshop versions prior to 7) with black as the foreground color to clear out the eyeball right to the edge of the eyelids.

So, I then had a single masked layer of the image with the eye cleared out, ready to have more layers added beneath it to help compose the socket. I initially struggled to come up with a viable solution to creating the eye socket. My main concerns were conveying the right amount of depth and also adding some type of organic texture inside the socket. I wanted the texture to be visible but very subtle, so that the viewer had to almost strain to notice it.

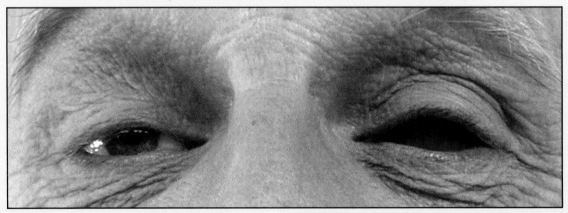

I started building the socket by creating a layer below the masked layer and filling it with a dark red color that I sampled from a portion of Charlie's skin that was in shadow. I created another layer on top of that (still below the masked layer) and used black paint with a large, soft brush to airbrush in the shading. Imagining the way that light would enter the eye socket, I made the shadowing darker toward the top of the socket and gradually lighter toward the bottom. Next, to utilize the red tint from the layer below, I set this layer's blending mode to Multiply, which combined the black shadow with the red tint to give the socket a fleshy tone.

Taking a step back and evaluating the composition, I determined that the shadowing wasn't dark enough, so I duplicated the shadow layer and left it set to Multiply. This was a little too dark, so I reduced the layer opacity down to 60%. Now that I was happy with the shadow and coloring of the socket, it was time to figure out how to go about finding the perfect texture for the socket.

It's often better to sample from the source than to try to create something from scratch. Charlie's face had some areas that were suitable to grab textures from – but none greater than the skin around his eyes. So, I ended up picking the area just above Charlie's right eye and creating a selection considerably bigger than the size of the eye socket area.

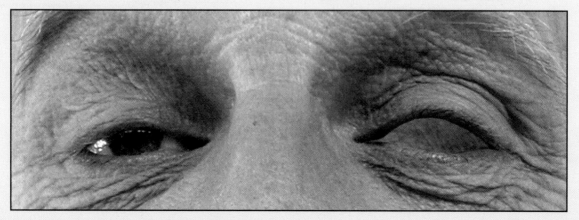

With the masked layer active, I created a new layer from the selection and then moved it just below the masked layer, making sure to also move it over so that it showed through the masked eye socket. To ensure that it wasn't obvious that I sampled the layer, I flipped it horizontally and vertically.

Currently, the skin texture is not subtle in the least. It's actually covering the other layers that make up the shadowing and skin tone. To blend the texture with the other layers below, I set the layer blending mode to Overlay, and reduced the opacity to 80%.

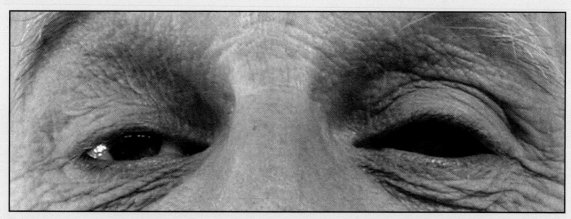

The composition is finally coming together, but there are a few areas that require some extra attention. First of all, I thought that the coloring of the eye socket was too strong – the red tint was too unrealistic. To combat this, I added a Hue/Saturation adjustment layer just above the layer filled with the red and set the Saturation to –75. This helped to make the image look much more real – if the socket was truly in so much shadow then there wouldn't be very much color visible.

The next fix was to tighten up the edges of the eyelid around the empty socket. My initial masking at the beginning wasn't quite precise enough. Against the darkness of the socket, it was clearly obvious that the edges of the eyelids required more masking as well as darkening. So, after cleaning up the mask, I created a new layer above everything and airbrushed a very soft black shadow on the edges of the eyelids. To blend it I set the layer blending mode to Soft Light.

The image is now complete – the socket is believable and the eyelid has been corrected to blend better with the now dark area that it encloses. The final touch of darkening the eyelid edges ensured consistency and tightened everything up.

Well, I call it finished, but this image has a problem – if an eye socket was truly missing an eyeball, the lid wouldn't have any form to it. It would most likely just be closed, or in the way I imagine it (which means more creepy), the lids would eventually grow together and close off the socket.

To achieve this effect I first decided to switch over and use the left eye, because there was more flat visible eyelid available to clone from. So starting over from the original photo, I first created a selection around the upper part of the top eyelid with the Lasso tool, and feathered it a bit. I then copied the selection as a new layer and moved it down as well as rotating it counterclockwise a little. The point of doing this was to match the curvature of the socket, and begin a process of gradually selecting pieces of the eyelid, and copying them as a new layer.

Weirdly, this felt like conducting reconstructive surgery – sometimes it's easier to come up with practical solutions if you think in the context of real world scenarios. So, what I basically did to finish the base of the effect was continue selecting more uniform areas of the lids (top and bottom), and then move and rotate them to cover the open part of the socket.

Once the base was done, I linked all the pieces of eyelid cover together and created a single flattened layer copy of the linked layers by holding down OPTION/ALT and selecting Merge Linked from the Layers palette. I knew I probably wouldn't have to use the linked pieces again, but I find it good practice to always account for as much flexibility as possible. Next, I hid all the linked eyelid pieces since I would be working with the single layer copy now.

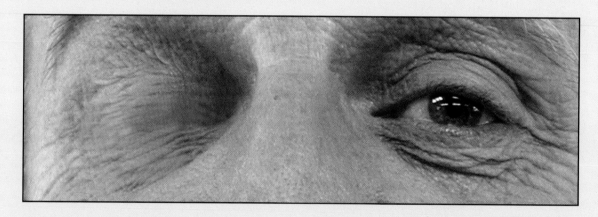

Naturally, the pieces don't mesh very well, so this is where the Stamp tool was useful. I went through the layer and used the Stamp tool to touch up the areas that looked too 'duplicated' (the patterned look you get with repeated layer copying), so I grabbed random areas to blend the wrinkles more seamlessly. I used the Stamp tool at 50% opacity to make the blending look smoother.

Here we have my wife Ashley, whose eyes have unfortunately turned into solid black orbs. This unsettling image's effects are relatively unsubtle compared to others in this chapter. However, the challenge with this portrait was to have the new eyes match the conditions of the rest of the image while preserving overall consistency. I chose this particular image for this effect because I felt dark eyes would contrast well with her light complexion.

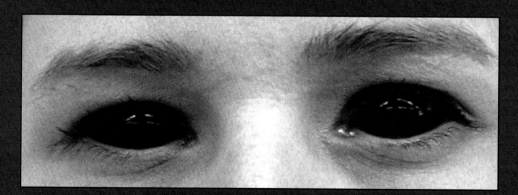

The initial and most basic thing I did to create the effect was building the base of the dark eyes. There were several approaches I could have chosen to achieve this such as drawing a selection around the exposed part of the eyeball and filling it black. However, I didn't like that option because it wouldn't allow me much flexibility, and I also wanted to use the existing reflections at the top of the eye.

Instead, I chose to paint the black in with the Airbrush, mostly because I prefer to use a freehand approach to applying effects (especially when using the Airbrush). Working on a new layer, I used a medium sized brush (around 40 pixels) with 50% Hardness to paint the bulk of the dark base. I left the pupil alone, and brushed over the iris, making sure to airbrush around the reflections.

Next, I could have easily just brushed in the entire area of the eye and used the Airbrush to recreate the reflections by hand. However, I wanted to preserve as much of the original conditions of the eye as possible, and the reflection of the lights at the top of the eye is one of the most important elements that contributes to keeping the eye looking realistic.

Most important was accurately airbrushing the black color right to the edge of the eye. If the black coloring was not close enough to the edges, then white of the eye would show through and the effect would look unrealistic. Similarly, if I painted too far beyond the boundary of the eye, I would encroach upon the edge of the eyelid. So, the main criteria to achieving this effect was accurately coloring inside the lines, just like the good old days of preschool.

The composition looks reasonable, but to help add a bit more realism I simply airbrushed in a very subtle inner glow to help give the impression that a small amount of light had entered the eyes. So, working on a new layer for each eye using a medium sized brush with 0% Hardness, I softly brushed in the highlight with white paint for each eye. As the highlights were too strong in their initial application, I used Gaussian Blur to soften them up a little and reduced the opacity way down to around 20%.

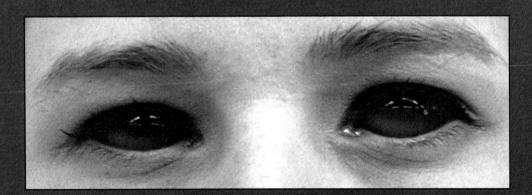

The composition is now at a point where I can almost accept that it's complete. One thing that I felt still needed some attention was the area around the eyes that are part of the original composition. If Ashley's eyes truly were solid black, the area around the eyes would be darker as well. My first instinct is to use the Burn tool to quickly darken up the eyelids, but instead I created a new layer and used the Airbrush to paint in the darkness around the eyes with black paint. I brushed it in very softly, and since I didn't necessarily want to apply black paint but to just darken the lids, I set the layer blending mode to Multiply and the opacity to 40%.

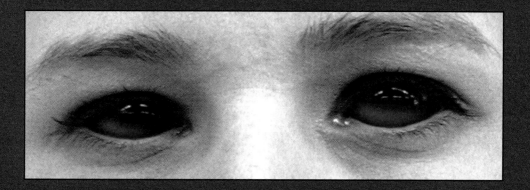

With these seemingly minor finishing touches in place, the composition is now complete. I discovered several issues myself working with this image – I originally thought I would be finished once I darkened the eyes and added the inner glow. After adding the final touches, though, it becomes apparent that you need to apply other subtle effects. These contribute to the overall realistic feel of the feature you are working on, in its wider context of the face.

If you think you've seen an intense glare from someone before, try to imagine that person glaring at you without any irises. Fabio's portrait manipulation – almost the exact opposite of Ashley's, was an easy choice because it contrasted exceptionally well with his dark complexion. Initially the eyes were solid white, but the addition of the pupils helped to create an intensity that was lacking.

To clarify, the process described here will be for one eye, but keep in mind that I used basically the same procedure for each eye. I stored all the layers for each individual eye in its own folder to keep everything separate.

I began manipulating Fabio's image by building a color base over his existing eyes. My first instinct was to select white and start airbrushing over the eye, but remember that you can achieve a higher degree of realism if you sample from the original. I opted to use the Eyedropper tool and sampled the shade of white from one corner of his eye and added it to the Swatches palette. I repeated this process for the other eye.

Next, based on these two shades of white I used the Gradient tool to create a gradated area of color above the eye on a new layer (in an area larger than the shape of the eye – I'm going to be adding a mask). Assuming there was no iris or pupil, I was trying to simulate the approximate range of color for the white of the eye.

Now that I have this swatch of color for the base of the new eye, I can add a mask to it and mask out the swatch to match the outline of the eye. I mask right to the edge of the eyelids (again using the mask icon in the layers palette, with the Airbrush and black foreground color) so that it now looks like Fabio has a flat off-white eyeball. I also mask back far enough so that the original whites of the eyes show through in the corners. There's no point wasting time recreating what already accurately and realistically exists in the image – after all, the only part I need to cover is the pupils and irises, right?

We've now got a solid base to work from – it's based on the actual color of the whites of his eyes and since it's masked, we have complete flexibility to add or subtract to it should we need to later on.

Now came the fun part – adding the assortment of reflections, shadows, and inner glows that a solid white eyeball would undoubtedly pick up. I wanted to work from the inside out, or to phrase it from a Photoshop perspective, from the bottom up. The first thing I set out to do was create an inner glow to add depth and roundness to the eye. Working on a new layer above the off-white base, I used a soft airbrush with white paint to softly brush in the glow/highlight in the lower left-hand corner of the eye. To make it ultra soft and give the eyeball a smoother feel, I used a Gaussian Blur to soften up the highlight.

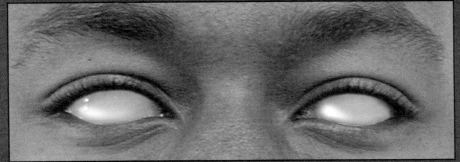

To contrast the soft inner glow, I needed to add sharper highlights to bring the eyes into focus. Working on a new layer above the base and inner glow layers, I used a smaller brush with medium Hardness and white paint to mimic the reflections that appeared on the eye in the original shot. I would have liked to sample the reflections in the original shot and reuse them, but since they appeared over the dark irises and pupils they were of no use. I also added very subtle highlights to the bottom edge of the eyeball to draw it out a little from the edge of the eyelid.

With all of the highlights in place it was now time to add some shadows. Taking cues from the original shot, it was clear I needed to add a strong shadow to the top of the eyeball because a strong shadow was being cast from the upper eyelid and lashes. I also determined that I needed to add a soft, subtle shadow to the bottom of the eyeball to give it added depth and separation from the bottom lid.

I used a soft black brush and airbrushed each shadow on its own layer, which were placed in between the highlights and the inner glow layers. I left the top shadows at 100% Opacity and Normal blending mode, but the bottom shadow needed to be reduced to 50% Opacity and set to Darken.

At this point I was pretty happy with the result, but couldn't let it go. There needed to be something else going on – it was a cool effect but lacked the extra touch of freakiness that I was looking for. To remedy this, I decided to add some pupils.

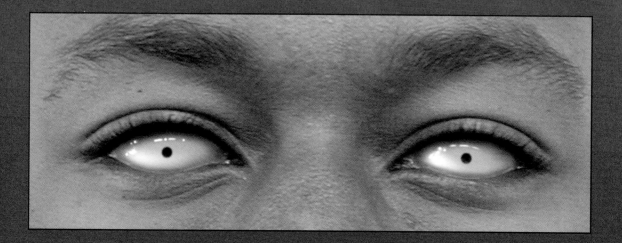

The process was fairly simple – I used the Elliptical Marquee tool to draw a circle and fill it with black. By itself that looked way too simple, so again I went back to the original image and looked for a hint on how to add a touch of reality to the pupil. It turned out that the pupil in the original shot had a slight dark glow around it, so I duplicated the pupil that I'd created and used a Gaussian Blur to soften it slightly.

The extra effort seemed to pay off – the final image is both subtle and striking, while the process of creating it was a lesson in taking cues from the original image when creating special effects.

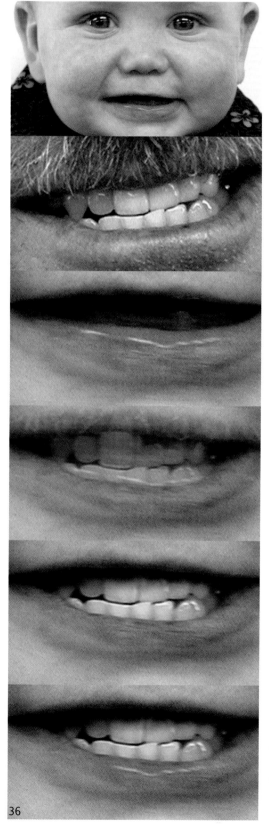

The casual browser might see Jake's finished portrait and wonder if anything has even been changed. However, the fact that Jake is an eight-month-old child should tip you to the fact that he shouldn't have a full set of teeth yet. The challenge with Jake's portrait was to realistically blend the teeth taken from another portrait, which happen to be the teeth of a 53-year-old man.

On the surface it wouldn't appear that there would be much work required to create this image. Simply sample the teeth from one image and drop them on Jake's face – perhaps a little cleanup, and it's all done, right? Well, there were actually a few more crucial steps involved that really pulled the composition together and made the effect blend in perfectly.

First, let's go back to the beginning – I determined that I wanted to use the teeth from a portrait of a 53-year-old man to replace Jake's one tooth mouth, since they both appear to have a slight underbite. Additionally, I thought it would be even more interesting to feature the drastic age difference between Jake (8 months old) and the teeth he would borrow from Tom (53 years old).

So, working on the image of Tom, I created a selection around his mouth, leaving plenty of room around the edges. I didn't worry about feathering the selection, as I knew I was going to end up masking it anyway. With the selection drawn, I moved the selected area of the image over to Jake's canvas, where it was naturally placed on top of the layer of Jake's portrait.

As I previously mentioned, I added a mask to the layer with Tom's teeth. Before I started drawing on the mask, though, I set the layer to 50% Opacity and moved it into the correct position over Jake's mouth. I needed to scale it down slightly to match the approximate shape of Jake's mouth. With Tom's teeth layer in place and still set at 50% Opacity, I began airbrushing on the mask with black paint right to the edges of Tom's teeth. When I was happy with the mask, I set the opacity of the layer back to 100% to get a true sense of where I stood. With everything looking good, it was time to apply the minor tweaks to finish off the image.

The first thing that bothered me was the color of the teeth. They were a little too yellow to be the teeth of a baby, so I had to make them a little whiter. The solution to this was to add a Color Balance adjustment layer just above the teeth layer, and move the bottom slider of the Midtones away from Yellow and toward Blue. I grouped the adjustment layer with the teeth layer to ensure that it only affected the teeth layer.

To introduce a little more realism to the image, I borrowed some of the original glare from Jake's bottom lip that had been covered by his new teeth and placed it on the portion of the lip that was now visible. This was a simple task of creating a selection around the glare on the original layer, feathering the selection and then creating a new layer from the selection. This new layer was then positioned over the bottom lip. I ended up adding a mask to the glare layer so that I could feather it even more, helping it to blend a little better.

This composition demonstrates that even the simplest of effects can always be improved by taking notice of small details and what can be added or modified to make that simple effect blend more seamlessly.

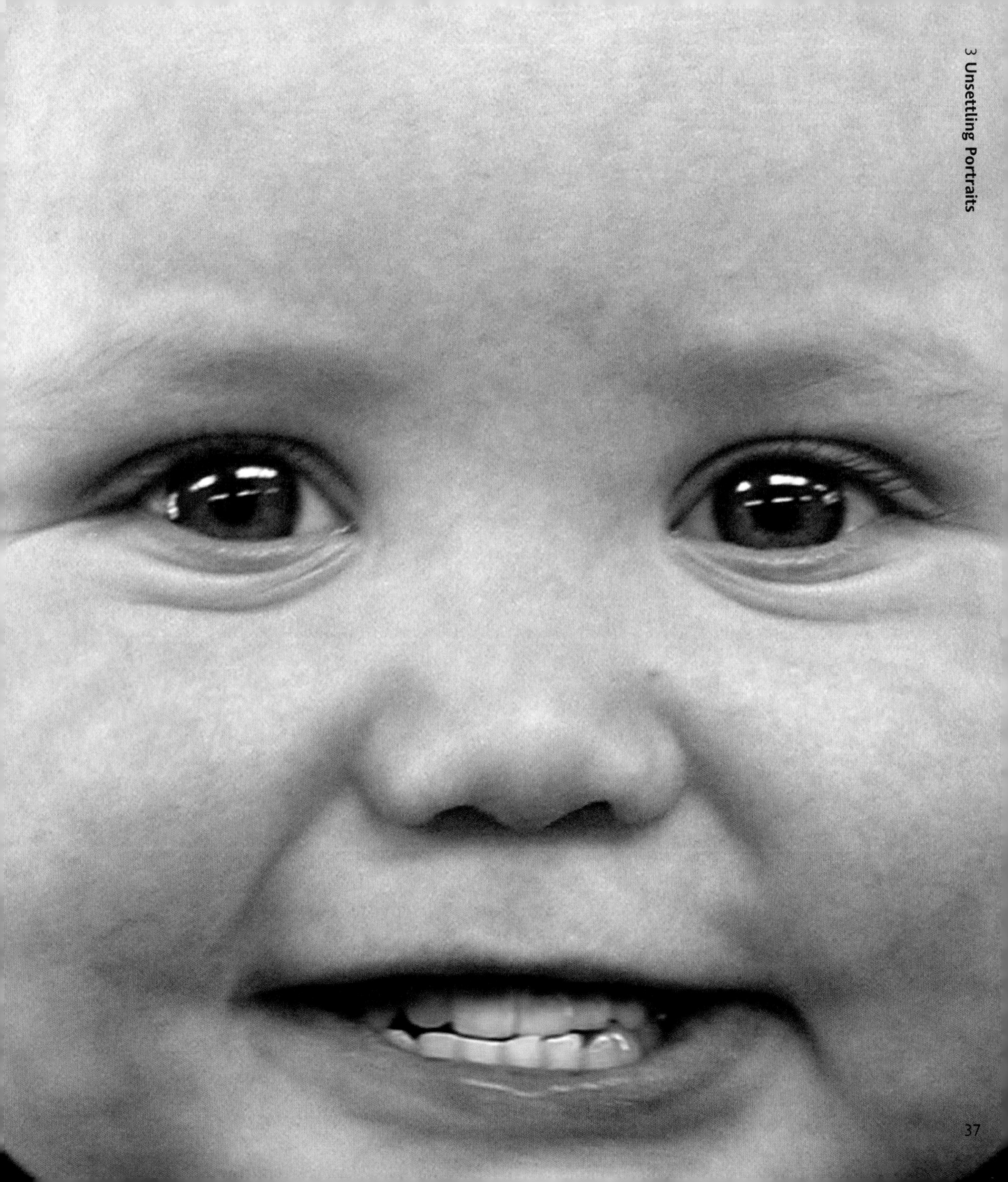

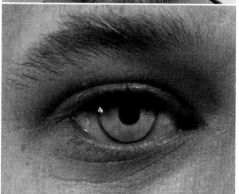

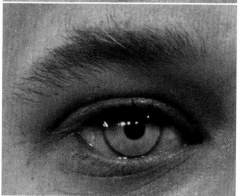

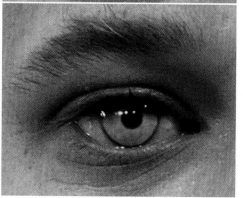

What I wanted to do here was make it look as if someone had replaced my normally clear contact lenses with those of Marilyn Manson. Plus, what happened to all my hair? No wait – that's my normal do. The major challenge with this effect was that I had such a small area to work in (the area between the pupil and edge of the iris). Additionally, I had to find an effective way to turn the iris of my eye clear while maintaining its edge. The techniques I described here will be for just the left eye, although I used the same procedure on each.

The main task with this composition was to change the iris of my eye to the same color as the white of my eye. I wanted to maintain the same little imperfections and color variations that were present in the visible white part of the eye in the iris that I was going to create, so I'd obviously be using the Clone Stamp tool, and sample from the left and right edges of the eye. Or was I?

With such a small area to work with, it would be a nightmare to try and use the Clone Stamp tool accurately. Alternatively, I opted to use the Lasso tool and draw a selection around the light, lower area of the left part of the white of my eye. Next, I feathered the selection a few pixels and created a new layer from the selection. I then duplicated and moved this new layer several times – enough to cover the iris. I wasn't worried about covering the edges of the iris or pupil at this point, as I planned to merge all the layers that made up the iris cover and then add a mask to it.

With the mask in place, I could now accurately use the Airbrush to mask the iris cover right to the edges of the original eye's iris, and right to the edges of the original eye's pupil. I now had a pretty seamless looking base to work from. As a result of the iris base covering some of the elements of the original iris, I now had to recreate the highlights and shadowing of the eyeball.

The first item I addressed was recreating the highlights: working on a new layer above the iris cover, I used the Airbrush with white paint and a small brush to paint in the highlights. I set the iris cover to 50% so that I could use the original highlights as a guide. Yeah, I guess you could say I was tracing them...

Once the highlights were drawn, I needed to add the shadows at the top and bottom of the eye to give the eyeball depth. Working on a new layer above the iris cover and below the highlights, I used a medium sized, soft brush to airbrush in the shadows at the top and bottom of the eye. To blend it with the eyelids and the rest of the eye, I set the layer blending mode to Darken.

There was still one aspect of the eyes that looked awkward to me at this point. The irises look fine, and blend well with the rest of the composition. The highlights and shadows also blended well and looked natural. However, the pupils now look odd, and I figured out that they looked unnatural because they were too well defined. I referred back to the original image to see how the pupils should look, and zooming in on one I could see that they have a somewhat irregular edge. Rather than trying to replicate this look, I borrowed straight from the source as I did so often throughout this series of portraits. So, I used the Elliptical Marquee tool to create a selection around an area just larger than the original pupils. I then created a new layer from the selection, and moved the layer just above the iris base. The final touch was to mask the layer, airbrushed with black until the new pupil was perfectly blended with the iris base.

This final touch sealed the deal, and showed again that sometimes all it takes is very minor touches to increase the realism and believability of a composition.

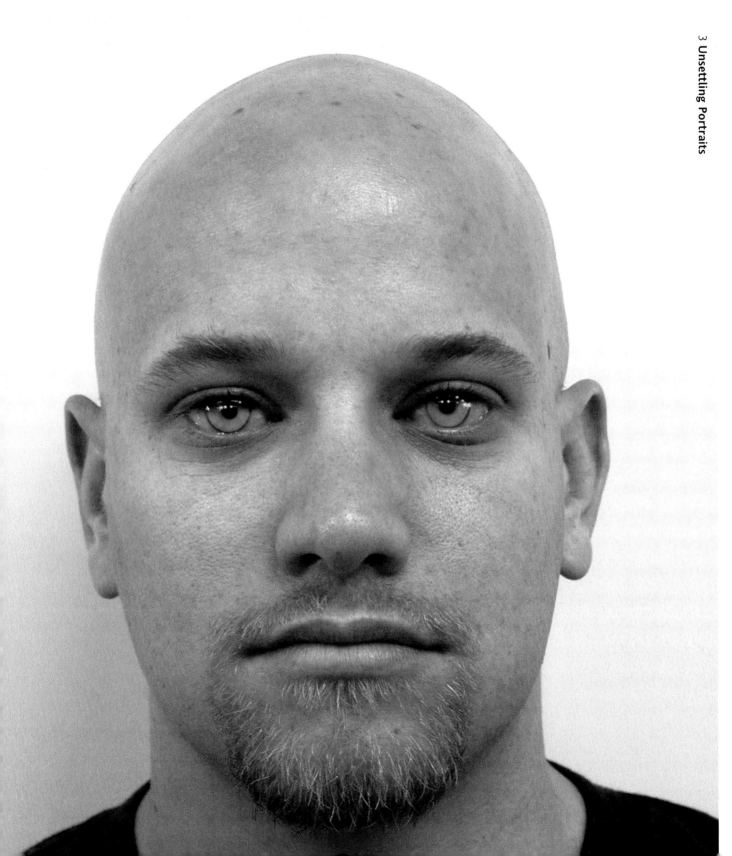

My mom Linda is probably going to hate me for creating this image. Giving her Medusa-like eyelashes was certainly a challenge, and it most likely couldn't have been done with a standard mouse. This effect is a huge plug for using a pen and tablet, which made it possible to airbrush the smooth strokes required to create the extended lashes.

This was possibly the most fun image to create, because of the intense amount of freehand drawing involved. Broken down, the effect is really very simple; it was just a matter of keeping a steady hand – which I didn't have. I had to constantly back up and start over several times, but that's just part of the process. Have you ever drawn a detailed image on paper without having to erase? Think of it that way.

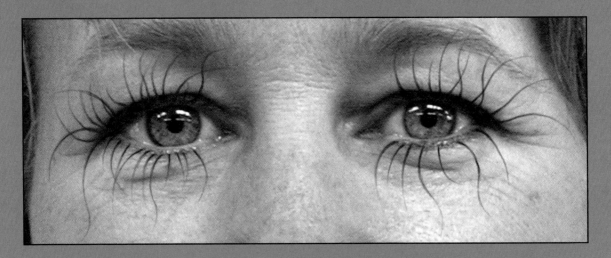

OK, down to business. I started out each set of eyelashes by simply creating a new layer and using a 1-pixel brush to airbrush in the lashes with solid black. I paid special attention to ensure each lash started out with a thick base and gradually tapered out to a fine point. The pen and tablet played a huge role here – they allowed me to create natural, sweeping strokes that would have been near impossible with a mouse. As a test, I tried creating the same lashes with my mouse, and the results were far less than spectacular. The mouse strokes were too short and inconsistent – I couldn't get near to the fluid strokes I created with the pen.

So, with a solid set of lashes brushed in (although it took a good hour or so to get everything right), I was ready to move on to the next step in bringing the lashes to life, so I studied the existing lashes to see how they reflected light and showed other colors. I could see that they had a hint of brown in them – a feature that added depth as well as color. To replicate this effect, I used the Eyedropper tool to sample the brown from the original lashes, and working on a new layer above the original lashes I used the same 1 pixel airbrush from before to paint in the brown color hues. I drew them into random places on the lashes – mostly around the edges and closer to the roots.

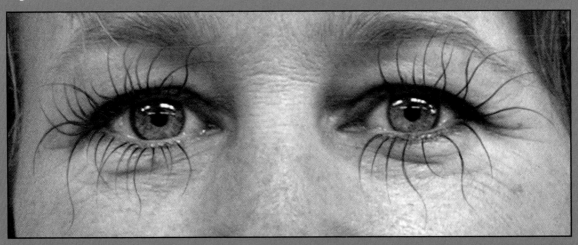

The next thing I noticed about the original lashes was that they did have individual highlights. So, in much the same manner that I created the brown tints on the lashes, I used the 1 pixel brush again on a new layer above everything else, except using white paint to airbrush in the highlights on the lashes. Additionally, instead of drawing on the edges of the lashes, I drew the highlights on the middle of the lashes. I also put the highlights in random sections, which helped emphasize that the lashes were really out of control and reflecting light at all different angles.

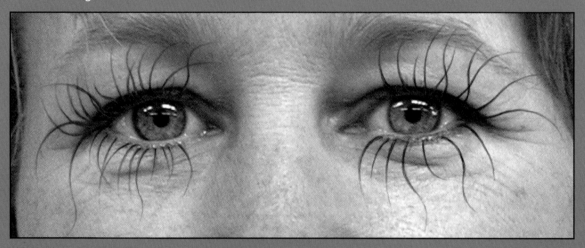

After completing these major steps, I still felt that the lashes weren't strong enough, and didn't quite gel with the rest of the image. To address the first concern, I simply duplicated the base layer of the lashes (the black one), which helped emphasize them more considerably. It was a little too much, though, so I reduced the opacity of the duplicate down to 50%.

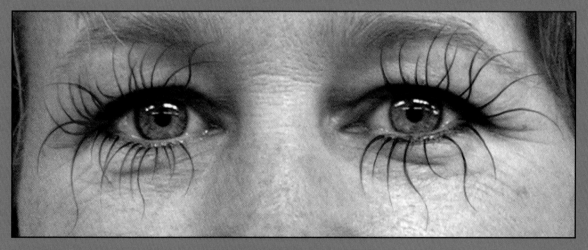

To pull the lashes together with the rest of the image a little better, I decided I was going to give them a very subtle shadow. I achieved this by duplicating the base lashes again, and moving the duplicate layer below the base lashes. Next, I applied a Gaussian Blur to soften the strokes and moved the layer slightly so the shadow looked offset a little. I then reduced the opacity down to 40% to achieve the subtlety that I was looking for.

The composition is now complete, and although the description makes it sound like a quick process, achieving a realistic effect was a very time-consuming process.

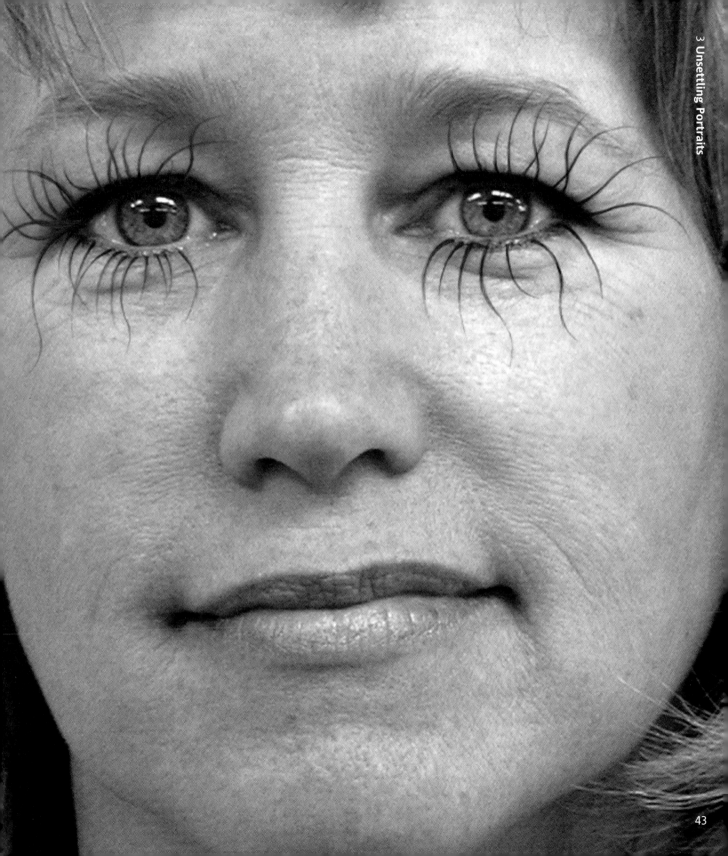

43

You really have to look hard to find the effect in Peter's portrait. Here's a hint: take a look at the moles and wrinkles on his face. You should be able to see that his face in the finished portrait is perfectly symmetrical, right down to the hair on his head. I initially thought that the challenge with this effect would be to make it look realistic, but it works surprisingly well with Peter's portrait.

The first thing I needed to do to get Peter's portrait ready for the effect was get his face perfectly straight – getting it as symmetrical as possible, with the eyes level and nose straight up and down. Otherwise, when I reflected one of the halves of his face nothing would match up right. The best way I found to do this accurately is to use the Measure tool and draw a line from the center of one pupil to the other. Then, when you go to **Image > Rotate Canvas > Arbitrary**, the rotation value that's necessary to rotate the image and make the eyes perfectly horizontal is automatically entered for you. I've had to use this technique from time to time and it works flawlessly as long as you have two distinct reference points.

Now that I had a somewhat symmetrical face to work with, the next thing I did was to add a mask to the layer and mask the right-hand side of the face. I used a large, soft brush, and didn't mask right up to the center line of the face because I wanted to have some space to work with, since I figured the edges wouldn't match up perfectly.

With the left-hand side of the face ready to go, I duplicated it and then flipped it horizontally. Now I had both halves of the face and it was just a matter of realistically matching them up. I could afford to be a little less than perfect since I had a little 'slack' on either side of the face's center.

With both sides of the face lined up, I highlighted the mask on the right side of the face and used the airbrush with a large, soft brush to go in and slowly mask out the extra slack that in some places was overlapping the left side of the face. Most of the work had to be done in the hair at the top of the head – it was really important to have that appear perfectly symmetrical. I didn't want the effect to be so perfect that it didn't even look like an artificial person. The neck also needed a lot of work, as there were very subtle color shifts that didn't quite match up right from the outset.

So, although this effect will probably go unnoticed by the majority of people, if you have a sharp eye you should be able to recognize the symmetry of this 'too perfect' face.

Up to this point, I've focused on one specific effect on each portrait. Here is a chance to see a portrait with several effects applied, and create a true freak of nature. Let's go back to the image of Jake, my favorite portrait. There's no need to revisit the descriptions of the effects here, but just to be aware that I used the eye effects from Ashley's portrait, the symmetry effects from Peter's image, and borrowed the eyebrows from Charlie, while and chin stubble came from Peter. The end result gives quite a disturbing montage!

Whoa, Jake just aged about 25 years (and also looks like he's from another planet, to boot)!

## Summary

The entire process of creating these freaks was really enjoyable. The concept is so simple, yet it is a great exercise for anyone interested in Photoshop. We get down to the roots of why we use Photoshop – plain and simple – we just love to mess with photos! Additionally though, during the course of tinkering with these photos, we've learned a few important lessons to help make our tinkering that little bit more real:

- Refer to the original image to help accurately assess the composition of the feature you're manipulating.

- Always sample from the source, rather than attempting to create a feature or effect from scratch.

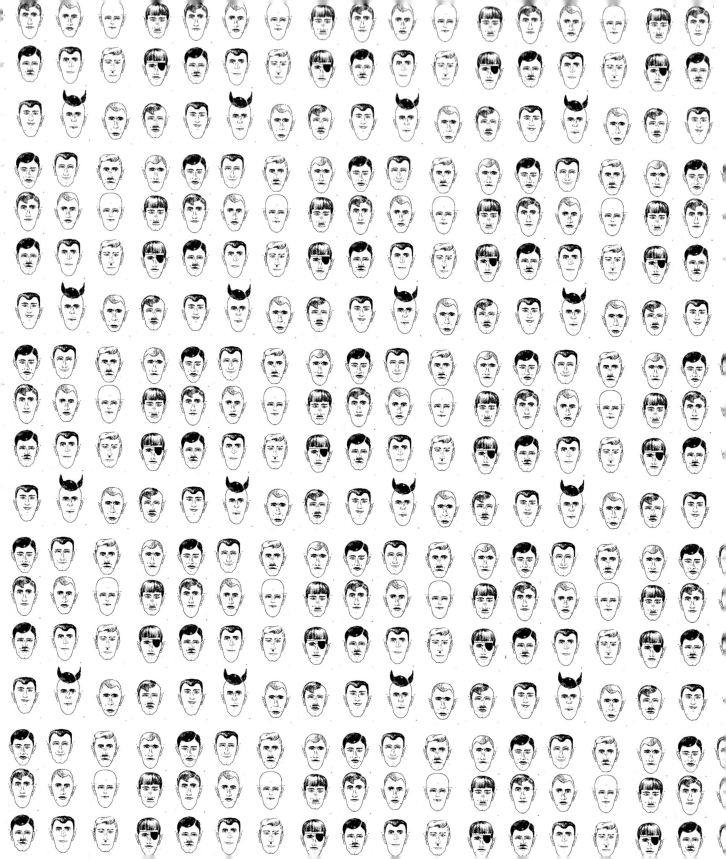

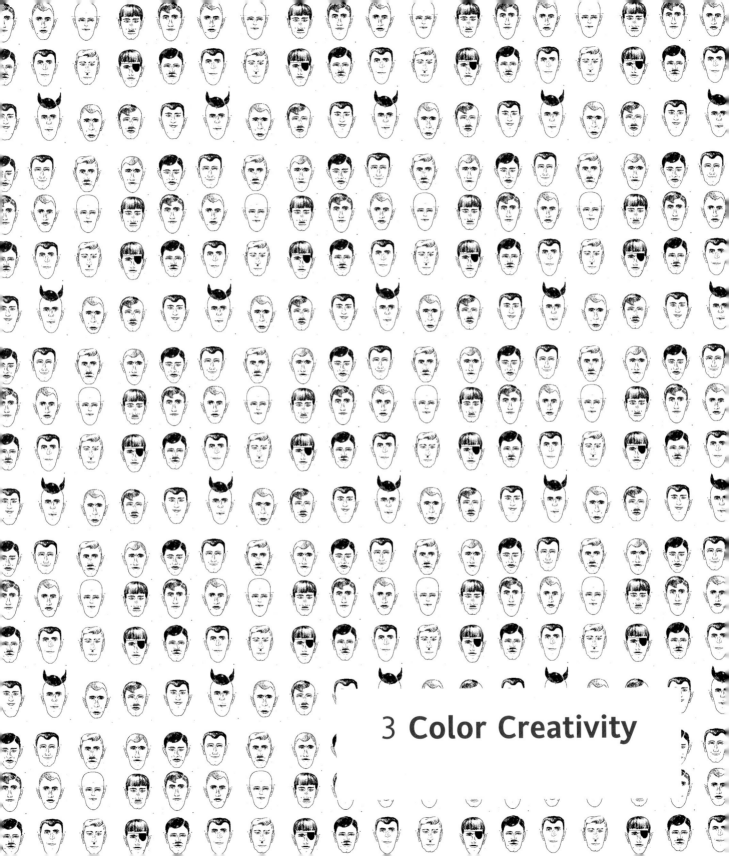

3 **Color Creativity**

This chapter is about color tools in Photoshop and how they can be used to help make faces look like they've had makeup applied to them. I'll focus on how it's possible to translate certain airbrush tools and Blending Modes into a professional makeup artist's makeup bag, containing the basics like eye shadow, mascara, and lipstick.

In my own work, I use the Airbrush to paint detailed portraits. I try to incorporate the philosophy that the airbrush is mechanical and erases flaws, forming a strange relationship between what is stylized and what is realism. The makeovers in this chapter are an extension of that type of work and its accompanying philosophy: the transformations have elements of realism while each one's goal is to attain a particular element of style or appearance.

For the past year, airbrush portraits have inspired my work. You can find airbrush portraits in many places, such as urban settlements, trucks, RVs/motor homes and clothing. The type of airbrush artistry that specifically interests me is the work that can be found on cars and t-shirts, mainly because it's small and detailed.

My affection for this work comes from growing up in Miami Beach and my familiarity with romanticized subject matter about sunny days and nightlife. I never get bored of seeing the same tiger icon, or famous people because the painting style is always unique. Airbrush is a difficult medium and I'm interested in noticing small mistakes as well as aesthetic decisions.

When I discovered Photoshop as a painting tool it opened many new opportunities for me. The digital element didn't affect the way I painted – it just felt natural. I was able to sketch and collage while going back through mistakes. I began to realize, though, that my painting was becoming very detailed because of the high degree of control I had over the Airbrush tool in Photoshop.

In this chapter, we'll be concentrating on how we can best optimize the airbrush control we have at our disposal in order to achieve the makeup effects we want – whether they're subtle or extreme.

## Sports fan

The dedication of certain sports fans is intriguing to me. Particularly, I'm thinking about sports fans who take the time to go out and buy paint, make a design for their face, and then sit uncomfortably with non-breathable paint on their faces for hours in the heat. It's a very theatrical and dramatic expression that has inspired my first makeover. This piece pays homage to the New York Mets – my favorite baseball team – and so, will include the colors blue and orange, along with a number 31 for catcher Mike Piazza.

As I wanted the paint application to look authentic, I studied some photos of painted fans partying at sporting events. Their makeup often looks sloppy and is often smeared. For me, some of the key elements of the 'sports fan makeover look' were messiness and sweatiness, in the name of your favorite team.

I guess, because of the extreme look of dedication mixed with a degree of messiness, I imagined this kind of fan to be over-excited and rowdy. To exaggerate the rough and rowdy element, I decided I would give our portrait a hockey player look, with bruises and a black eye to complement his face paint. Before any of the fun stuff, the image needs to be prepared.

With the image open in Photoshop, I selected the **Layer > New Adjustment Layer > Levels** menu option and chose the **Group With Previous Layer** option to group it with the previous layer containing the photo. Once the levels were ok, I adjusted the color balance, keeping the original photo handy to help accurately match colors and light.

The photo's dark background is really incongruous to the sports theme, so I added a new layer (ungrouped with any previous layers) and with the new layer selected, I clicked the Add Layer Mask icon at the bottom of the Layers palette. I then started to cut out the background using the Airbrush tool at 100% black. If you cut too much out, hitting the X key switches the color to white, helping you to regain any erased mistakes. Using my tablet with the 'pressure' option checked enables me to get a soft and realistic edge.

It's useful to make sure that the layer beneath the one you're cutting out is a bright, contrasting color, so you can clearly see whether you've erased everything. You can also keep track of the mask by making it red, holding down Opt/Alt-Shift and clicking on the layer mask thumbnail.

Anyway, I said we'd get on to the fun stuff. Let's start with that bruise. Having collected some pictures of cuts and bruises, I arranged them on the screen next to my canvas.

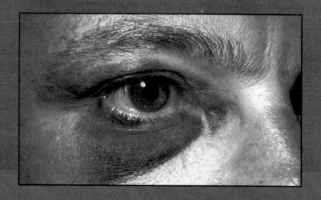

By using the Eyedropper tool on certain bruised color, I started to create a custom palette. I created a new canvas about 1 x 1" and used the Eyedropper tool to collect colors from my reference bruises. The color range of a black eye is limited to grays and browns, but fortunately the Eyedropper tool has the ability to select colors one pixel at a time. Utilizing the tool's high power of selectivity, I was able to steer away from 'muddy' tones and search for more high intensity secondary colors, selecting pure browns just for mixing.

It's possible to mix colors in normal blending mode by lightly tinting a color with the Airbrush, selecting the color with the Eyedropper, and saving it in a custom palette. I also used the web palette because I work in RGB and it has a basic range of color. With the RGB sliders it's easy to darken colors by adding the complimentary color. With the HSB sliders, you can subtract black from the color.

I located burnt umber and sienna; a warm olive and warm purple. Layering these colors lightly on top of dark browns would deepen the tone without making it muddy, as opposed to adding gray and black which can make an area dull and flat.

At this stage I checked out some sports fan reference pictures to assess how thickly they apply face paint. One common theme I noticed was it seemed usual to apply paint sloppily around the eye area without a distinct shape. Usually eyebrows were painted but there was often a gap in the paint where skin showed through underneath the eye area. This worked well for me, as it gave me enough space to focus on realistically incorporating a black eye.

I was now ready to start painting, so I added a new grouped layer at the top of the layer stack. In the Layer Style window, I selected Multiply from the Blend Mode drop-down menu. The Airbrush now acted as my makeup application brush and my custom palette acted as a compact eye shadow kit.

Multiply mode helped the brush stokes sit naturally around the contours of the eye by mixing the colors together. As this layer was grouped, Multiply mode combined new colors with existing colors in the photo to create a third, darker color. Any dark areas or lines on the skin were enhanced, which worked well towards achieving the effect of a black eye. I painted lightly, being careful not to over saturate the dark colors. Making slight marks helps add realistic light and energy to the surface, so I worked lightly from the ground up. With this in mind, I rarely used the Undo function, as my brush strokes quickly added up to the desired effect.

Here you can see how the strokes look in the context of the portrait as well as a single entity – fully showing the bruise-making process that's happened on top of the skin.

The next step was to add the actual face paint colors in a vertical half blue, half orange design. To help achieve this, I needed to make a mask of the face. I copied the photo layer and placed it at the top of the layer stack. The copy already contained a mask that was used to separate the photo from the background. In the mask layer, I continued to erase by using 100% black, cutting around the shape of the eyes and the face.

I wanted the paint around the eye areas to look smeared and faded, so I lowered the pressure and haphazardly erased.

The blending mode that best imitates light and dark is Overlay. When Overlay mode is painted on top of existing colors, it enhances contrast and helps boost color's saturation. I've found that this doesn't work so well with lighter skin because the color tends to over saturate. In this case, orange turns fluorescent yellow, blue turns iridescent purple.

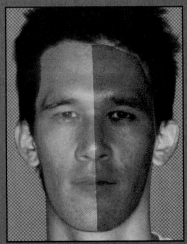

To resolve this, I chose to desaturate the color from the layer to give me a grayscale mask.

I added a new grouped layer named 'face color' and arranged it at the top of the layer stack with an Overlay Blend Mode. I made a vertical line straight down the face with the Polygonal Lasso tool, completing a shape to be filled in with orange and did the same for the other half of the face so that it could be colored with blue. Next, I went back to the mask layer with a white, low pressure Airbrush in order to return some skin texture and, in turn, color to the image. I experimented with adding and subtracting color density in the mask layer until I was happy with the amount of fading or thickness around the eye.

The final steps involved making the makeup look smeared, sloppy, and messy. He needed to look as if he'd been screaming in the hot sun all day and then got involved in a bar brawl at night. Back on the 'face paint' layer, I used the Smudge tool and made a gestured smear across the hard line of color in between the eyebrows. I wanted the smudge placed here in relation to the black eye to help accentuate battle scar evidence. Additionally, I went back to the mask and erased color underneath his eye to complete the appearance of a fist type motion that had swiped across his eye. I then further softened the harsh vertical division of color with the Smudge tool and Airbrush.

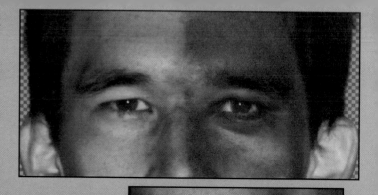

Finally, the cause of it all: Mike Piazza's number 31. I decided that the two digits were going to be white, but it was important that they looked dingy, dirty and tinted with both orange and blue. I switched to the HSB Sliders to easily add white to each color. In the 'face color' layer, I used the Airbrush at 25% Pressure and drew both numbers on, before softly painting the edges to help make them look grungier.

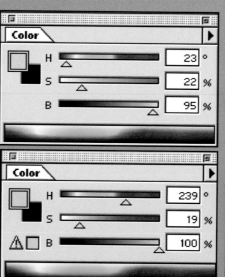

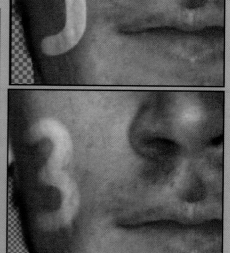

If you take a look at the mask images here, it will give you a good idea of the level of work I put into achieving the smearing and coloring effects.

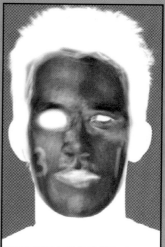

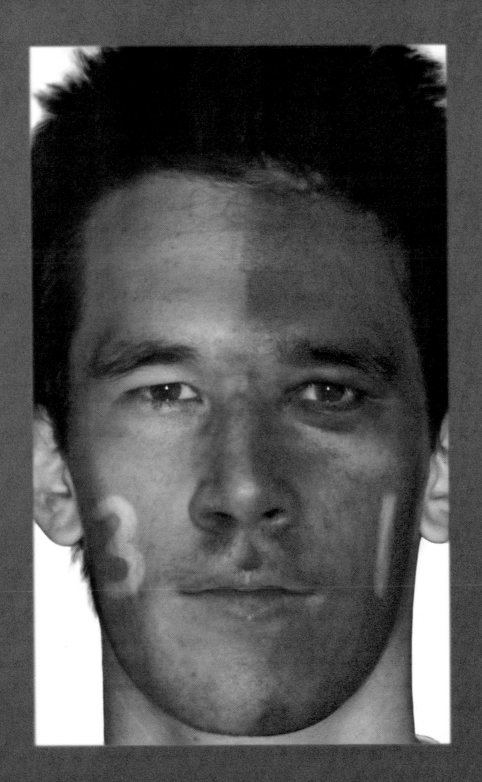

## Tigress

For this portrait, my focus was on experimenting with transforming a female into a tigress. Aside from being associated as being wild and exotic, tigers are also associated with glamor and wealth. The concept of a makeover as a mask can help introduce depth of content to a woman's portrait and convey traits or features that wouldn't necessarily be prominent in a standard picture.

My main aim in this makeover was to combine the 'wild sides' of both women and tigers. The dramatic stripes and dark outlines that you see around the eyes and mouth of a tiger would also really help to enhance female facial features. The combination of soft white and orange furry texture, combined with stark black was a fun juxtaposition to experiment with.

This photo was taken with 35mm 800 speed film that was pretty grainy. After I had the composition in place, I used the Despeckle Filter (**Filter > Noise > Despeckle**) in a bid to reduce the granularity slightly. This only had a subtle effect, but every little bit helps. Next, I added some Adjustment Layers, as you can see from the screenshot:

Additionally, because the background to this portrait was pretty unattractive, I added a layer mask and erased the background, naming this layer 'Miya mask'. I made a copy of 'Miya mask' and proceeded to erase around the shape of the face with 100% black. Next, I desaturated the photo using the same method as in the previous sports fan makeover. In this case, because of the poor quality photograph, the grayscale value needed more contrast. I added adjustment levels so that the light on her face would be visible underneath the Overlay paint, contributing to a more realistic effect. Experimenting with the contrast also helped to achieve a chalky texture, which I was looking for.

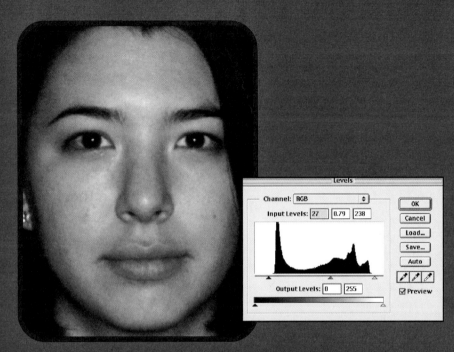

Adding a new grouped Overlay layer, I started sketching with color. I faintly painted an undercoat shape of white and tiger orange around the cheeks and also painted the lips pink – this acted as a reminder for me to keep realism at a distance and concentrate on a stylized and glamorous version of a tiger.

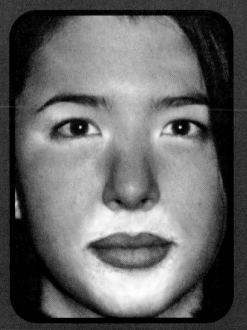

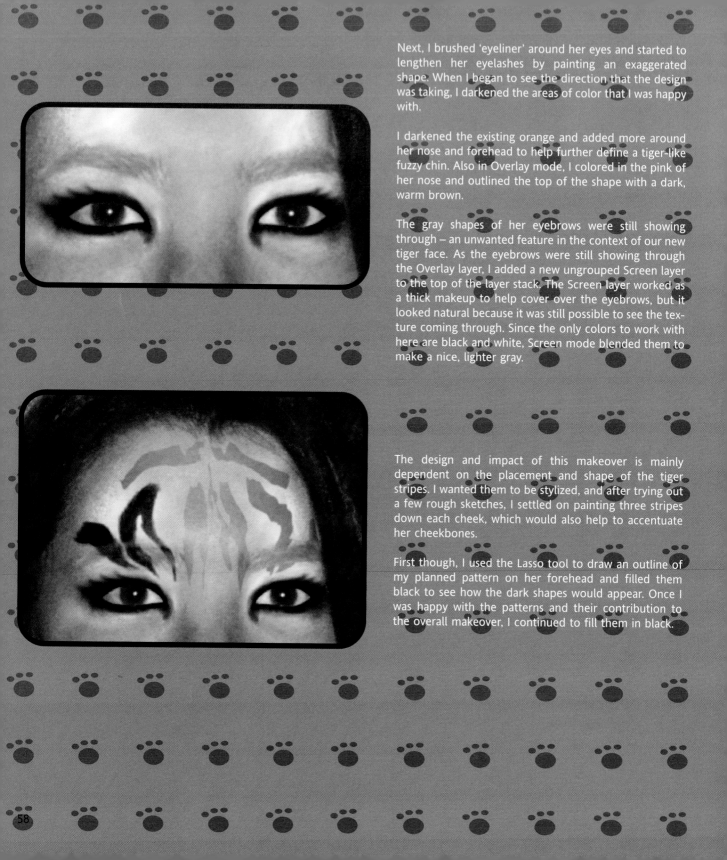

Next, I brushed 'eyeliner' around her eyes and started to lengthen her eyelashes by painting an exaggerated shape. When I began to see the direction that the design was taking, I darkened the areas of color that I was happy with.

I darkened the existing orange and added more around her nose and forehead to help further define a tiger-like fuzzy chin. Also in Overlay mode, I colored in the pink of her nose and outlined the top of the shape with a dark, warm brown.

The gray shapes of her eyebrows were still showing through – an unwanted feature in the context of our new tiger face. As the eyebrows were still showing through the Overlay layer, I added a new ungrouped Screen layer to the top of the layer stack. The Screen layer worked as a thick makeup to help cover over the eyebrows, but it looked natural because it was still possible to see the texture coming through. Since the only colors to work with here are black and white, Screen mode blended them to make a nice, lighter gray.

The design and impact of this makeover is mainly dependent on the placement and shape of the tiger stripes. I wanted them to be stylized, and after trying out a few rough sketches, I settled on painting three stripes down each cheek, which would also help to accentuate her cheekbones.

First though, I used the Lasso tool to draw an outline of my planned pattern on her forehead and filled them black to see how the dark shapes would appear. Once I was happy with the patterns and their contribution to the overall makeover, I continued to fill them in black.

The stripes on the cheek were a bit more difficult. They had to be equally positioned at the correct angle as well as being symmetrical to help achieve the look that I wanted. Before making the outline, I painted white lines as a guide on top of the orange that was already there. These act almost like white shadows that sit under the black.

Using the Lasso tool and trying to work along the curve of the cheek, I drew a jagged stripe, which became thinner towards the nose. I then painted the inside of the shape black using the Airbrush, but because there wasn't enough light and skin texture showing through on her cheeks, I added some white to help add softness to the pattern, and interrupt the flat black.

Next, I added a new layer to the top of the layer stack and made a layer mask. I needed to see what I was painting in the layer mask and at the same time, see the makeup to trace the stripes. Using OPT/SHIFT-CLICK, the new layer mask turns red and acts like a screen.

Using black, I painted out a mask of the stripes and made the layer Screen mode, before lightly retouching the stripes with white using a soft brush at 6% Pressure. More detail was added to the cheeks by blurring their edges and also adding an extra element of yellow with the Airbrush.

I also added different shades of pink to the lips – giving them more variation and body, and also helping them to appear more full. Simulating the application of lip liner helped to give a nice effect around the mouth area and helped to mimic the dark outline around a tiger's mouth. I'm a fan of extra dark lip liner that's specifically painted to stand out, rather than flawlessly blend with lipstick. This lipstick application is based on lipstick that is applied with a brush and then blended – I tried to take advantage of the pre-existing highlights on the photo and added bright white highlights on her lips to enhance natural shine.

I think you'll agree that was a pretty successful makeover. Combinations of both striking and subtle effects bind really well together to help achieve the female tigress appearance that I was looking for. Of course, if you want to go beyond simulating makeup application and really incorporate a tiger appearance, you could look at manipulating the eyes and mouth so that they have more feline characteristics. Along with the addition of a few whiskers, you'd really have something far flung from the original portrait.

# Clown

When I was a kid, my Mom would dress as a clown every year on Halloween. She was a drama teacher and very skilled at theater makeup. I always wanted her to paint my face like hers so I could see it transform. After seeing Eva's photo, I couldn't let the opportunity pass by to return to childhood memories. Eva's expression in this photo was precious; how could I ever possibly improve on such a perfect photo?

I had to paint an even more endearing personality – that of a young hobo clown.

This makeover is based purely on greasepaint and love. I thought the background looked great – sort of like a country setting that helped add a positive element to what would become a bittersweet character. After applying the same desaturation and mask techniques as the previous exercises, I created a new Overlay mode layer and started painting a peach tone on her forehead.

Before I decided on this color, I tried different tones on the Overlay layer by clicking Preserve Transparency at the top of the Layer palette, and pressing OPTION/ALT-SHIFT-DELETE (CTRL-BACKSPACE on a PC), to scroll through the selected foreground color.

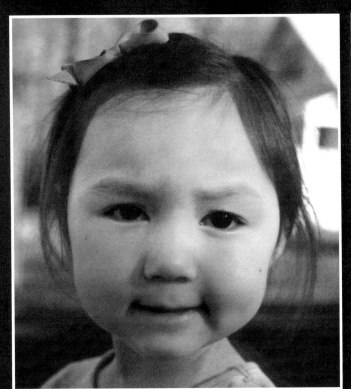

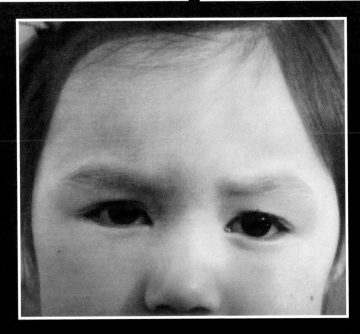

Eventually, I decided that the peach tone looked the best. I then painted around her eyes with white, which helped to give the makeup a powdery look. I started her beard by adding black under her nose with a soft brush at 40% Pressure, and continued the beard on her cheek and around the mouth. The appearance of the beard helped convey the look of a glum expression around the mouth area, which I accentuated by painting the inside white.

Her lips were still apparent in the Overlay mode, so I disguised them by adding more white on a new Screen layer. For this, I used a soft brush at 9% Pressure, being careful not to make the white look too opaque.

Back on the Overlay layer, I drew a red line on her bottom lip to further accentuate the look of a frowning face. I had to go back and erase some of the white on the Screen layer to prevent it interfering with the red line. Next, using a hard brush I painted her nose with the same deep red I used on her bottom lip, before powdering her cheeks with a softer brush and a slightly more cool, rosy red.

Finally, using a hard brush I applied black around her eyes like eyeliner, and also added some long, stylized eyelashes to give her the special girl clown touch — I wanted to make sure I brought attention to the fact that she's a girl clown, even though she has a beard! I finally added some out of position eyebrows, and our girl hobo clown was complete.

Eva's face now looks tinged with sadness, but is still captivating even though she's now wearing wacky clown makeup.

## New romantic

For this makeover, I was inspired by the 18th century fashions that were so evident in fashion and popular culture during the new romantic wave of the 1980s. I loved this era – when it was common and sexy for men, as well as women, to wear lavish makeup. My inspiration for this makeover can be related to Adam Ant, Falco, The Human League and Billy Idol.

When Jon's photo came back from the lab, his long hair and pouting face seemed to cry out for a glam makeover in the style of the pop artists just mentioned.

While the background of this photo is OK – Jon's hair is styled like a sculpture, so it would be a shame to have it camouflaged and hidden away. I thought having Jon's hair prominent in the portrait would help enhance a dramatic look.

I started off by going through the adjustment steps used in the previous exercises, as well as creating a mask to erase the hair. I think this approach adds a necessary handmade quality to an otherwise flat photograph. I probably place too much credence on this process than I should. I'm very aware of certain details in the work and, for me, hair is one of the most important. I guess I'm almost obsessive, but it would make me crazy to think that I didn't fully use my ability when it comes to painting. Although I'm aiming for realism, I still think as a painter and simply can't avoid wanting to add a personal touch to everything. I especially enjoy making visual discoveries along the way — seeing something new is so valuable because it helps the work develop and can give you so many new ideas and options.

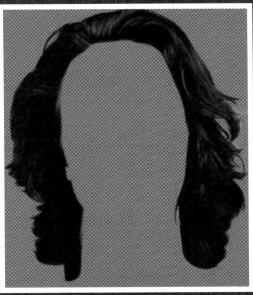

I put a layer of green underneath the photo/mask layer to help me see my progression more clearly. Once the hair was cut out, I copied that layer and erased his face to create a mask of his hair. I thought the Overlay mode worked well with coloring light and dark, so I desaturated the color from his hair. His hair had middle gray tones and not enough contrast, so I added a new grouped Levels Adjustment Layer. To add the color, I selected another new grouped layer with an Overlay blending mode. Using a soft brush at 50% pressure, I colored the hair with a sienna orange tone. I thought this effect looked realistic enough and I liked the subtlety of the orange because I wanted to achieve a slight orange tint. However, due to my obsession with getting features such as hair just right, I thought some highlights were a little over saturated. On a new grouped Multiply layer, I painted a few marks here and there to soften the saturation. I also enhanced dull areas by adding highlights in a new grouped Screen layer.

The effect of the Overlay layer was so far working great for applying thick colors to the skin. Since this is an 18th century/1980s hybrid makeover, the treatment for his eyes needed to be severe and dark, while the skin needed to be light and powdery.

Eye treatment was the main concentration in makeup of the 1980s new romantic era, while the rest of the face commanded less importance. The eye shadow around his eyes helps to define bone structure by making the eyes look slightly recessed into the face. So, in keeping with the new romantic focus of this makeover, it felt right that I should paint his eyes first and let the rest follow.

I copied the desaturated photo layer, deleted the hair mask and then added a Mask layer. By making the mask red, I painted black around the mouth and eyes – isolating them as gray shapes, and then deleted the rest.

I created a custom palette using the Eyedropper tool on some pictures of new romantic artists in order to replicate their exact makeup color – I started by borrowing a dark brown eye shadow and red lipstick color from a Billy Idol picture. In a new grouped Overlay layer, I lightly applied a sienna brown type eye shadow around his eyes, and a subtle red lipstick to his lips. The mask did most of the work for me – I mainly had to fill in the shape and let Overlay take care of maintaining the natural light of the photo. I accentuated his eyelashes with the Airbrush and a hard stroke of eyeliner around the eyes. Next, I applied reddish brown underneath the eyes, which provided a slight contrast to the top part of his eyelids.

This design is more artistically based, so my approach was to treat his face like a canvas and improvise. I added a new ungrouped layer and tried to paint in Normal mode, although this just covered over the photo. Selecting Screen mode, however, allowed the texture to remain. I painted lightly on his face with the Airbrush, using a skin foundation color I borrowed from a reference. I concentrated on defining his bone structure – patting color around his nose, chin, and cheeks. This was a slow application since I was still sketching at this point, but I didn't have any problems with the colors in Screen mode and was able to paint away happily.

I noticed that his eyebrows were getting lost, as they were pretty light to begin with. New romantic artists of the 1980s often had high arched, plucked eyebrows:

As Jon's eyebrows didn't give me much to work with, I had to give him some new ones. I drew them on the Screen layer as if I was using a makeup pencil. You can see that his eyebrows are now much better defined compared to how they were originally:

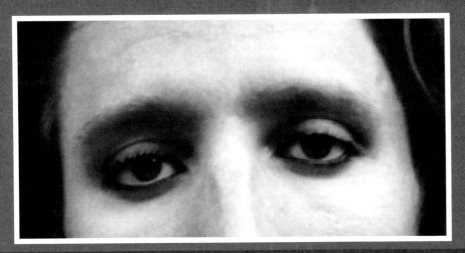

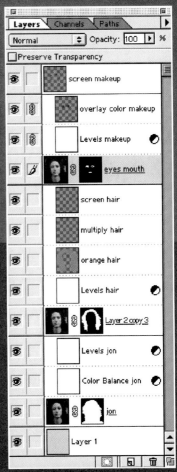

To powder his face, I used the Airbrush at a low pressure with a warm peach tone and light ochre. It was important to give him a gaunt and pouting presence, so I made sure that the darker tones further exaggerated his bone structure around the nose and chin. I sharply defined the shape of his lips with dark red on the Screen layer and retouched them with small white marks on the surface to add extra shine.

Another essential component for this makeover was the chiseled cheekbone. I painted a dark line down both cheeks and faded them out towards the eyes. I also painted a red line at an angle, which faded as it approached the mouth. I used the Airbrush like blush, working the strokes upward to make the cheeks look rosy and realistic.

Finally, he wasn't complete without a sassy heart and a beauty mark; reminiscent of Adam Ant. The mask here shows the core areas of manipulation that were made to Jon's face:

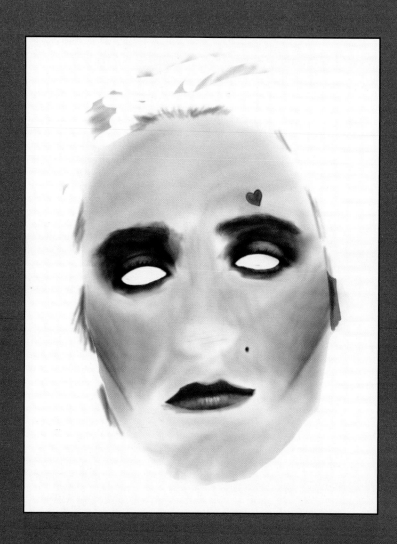

## Glossy magazine makeover

Airbrushing faces, or even entire bodies is common practice in print magazines. Whether intended to simply remove an unsightly spot, or maybe a sheen from someone's forehead or cheekbones – or indeed to do something more drastic – airbrushing in print media can look good or horrid. Perhaps a good way to differentiate is whether you actually notice that airbrushing has been applied or not. In this makeover of Barbara, I'll go through some techniques to help achieve competent and professional looking airbrush effects.

My idea for this makeover was to go all the way with makeup and make her face look like a painting. I looked at wedding photos for inspiration, particularly the well made up faces of bride's maids. I also looked at studio portraits, such as 'glamor shots'. Not only did the makeup techniques in these photos interest me, but I also found the blurry, soft lens element to be intriguing. I remember that my high school senior photo was airbrushed and it looked like I had makeup caked all over my face, when in actual fact, I was wearing none at all. So, I wanted to experiment and address all of these dramatic but conventional effects on Barbara because she has a very subtle and natural look.

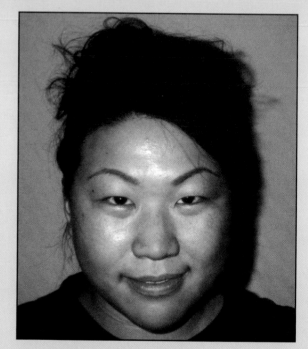

My intention was not to paint her face like a wacky beauty pageant contestant with blue eye shadow and hot pink lipstick; I just stuck with natural earth tones. Before starting to paint, I knew that this type of makeup treatment makes skin look unnaturally smooth and airbrushed, so I used the Stamp tool over all of the freckles and inconsistent areas in the photo.

I added Color Balance and Levels Adjustment Levels to balance the light in her face and then copied each of these layers to create a mask of her face with the correct adjustments. I thought this would make the application of the paint easier because I would mostly be using a large soft brush.

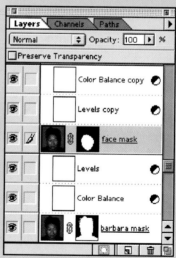

Using the Eyedropper tool on different areas of her face, I acquired a good range of tone to accentuate the lights and darks in the photo. Applying the paint had to be done in both Multiply and Screen Blending Modes. Combining Overlay with her skin color in the foreground resulted in a new saturated color, which I didn't want. When I applied a dark color in Screen mode, both dark hues cancelled each other out to produce a very light tone. A stroke of white applied with 100% Pressure in Multiply mode didn't show up at all, so I painted the darks in the Multiply layer and the lights in the Screen layer.

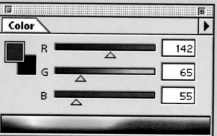

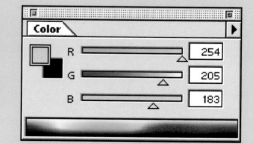

In the Screen layer, I dulled down her shiny spots, just like applying a makeup foundation. I used a soft brush at 15% Pressure very lightly to powder her cheeks, forehead, nose and chin, before adding a little extra right underneath the arch of her eyebrows.

In the Multiply layer, I used the brown tone and followed along the contours of her cheekbones with a slightly smaller soft brush. I slowly built up the color, trying to totally even out the skin to make the complexion look flawless. I used the brown eye shadow directly between her eyes and eyebrows.

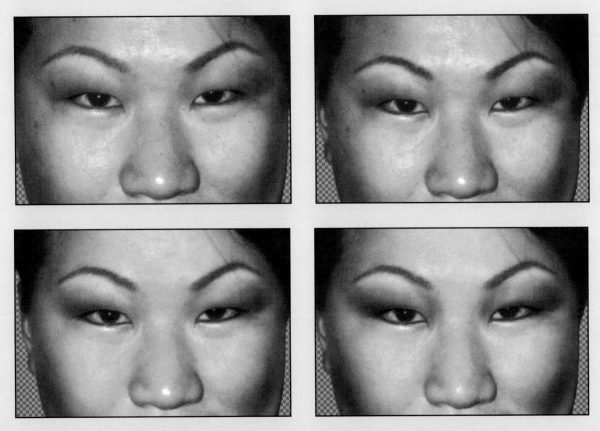

I noticed that many flattering and blurry photos have a white glowing effect, especially on the cheeks, forehead and nose. I really wanted to push this effect so that her skin looked as if it had been painted, so I painted strokes of a light tan color under her eyebrows. In the Multiply layer, I added a warm brown around her eyes and also darkened her eyebrows a little.

I also wanted her lipstick to look rich, as if it had been painted on, so I added a separate mask for her lips along with a Levels adjustment layer.

I first painted a red color that was too strong compared to the subtlety of her face, so I added a cooler red along with a small amount of purple, before making her lips look fuller with the application of some bright white.

I had already made a separate mask of just her face and I needed to apply some additional color manipulation on top of simply laying down airbrush marks on the surface of her skin. I readjusted the Color Balance layer, which helped me to even out the dull colors in her face. The lights became brighter and the dark areas evened out.

The shine on her forehead was difficult to eliminate. I worked in a Normal blending mode layer where I airbrushed the surface of her skin into a smooth texture. Using the Gaussian Blur filter with a 67.0 pixel radius on this layer, I was able to make the skin completely even and remove any evidence of brush strokes. This effect worked well – enabling me to regain some of the realistic shine from the photo rather than lightly erasing the marks.

Barbara's finished portrait certainly relates to some of the elements I mentioned when I started this makeover – she looks like she's wearing lots of make-up – perfect for a glossy wedding magazine or a high school senior yearbook.

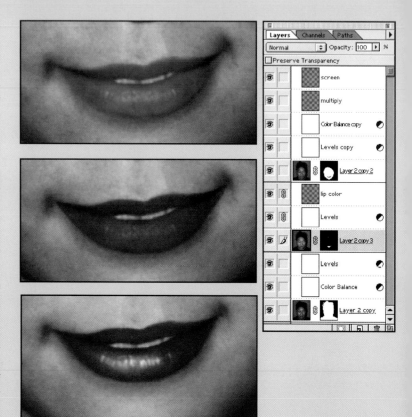

## Applying a simple lightning bolt across the face

For my last makeover, I worked in Overlay mode without having to desaturate skin tone. Whereas paint applied in Overlay mode tended to over saturate on light skin, it was enhanced as it mixed with Kymar's darker skin tone. The makeover will be a vivid blend of colors that are very effective and it's easy to do, with the right foreground color.

For this design I wanted to replicate a makeover in the ilk of a 1970s glam rock star and looked at pictures of music artists such as David Bowie, Kiss and the New York Dolls.

As I'd already experimented with thick paint, I was curious to see how fluorescent color would look with a light application. David Bowie's Aladdin Sane image combined a design element like that of the wrestler Ultimate Warrior, as well as addressing the delicacy and glamor of 1970s fashion.

I first added Color Balance and Levels Adjustment Layers before adding a new grouped Overlay layer. In the Overlay layer, using a brush at about 13% Pressure, I started painting with red along the edges of his face. I thought the glowing effect suited the concept for this makeover quite well, so I used the same brush in Overlay and checked my Aladdin Sane reference to draw the lightning bolt across his face.

In a new Screen layer that I grouped and placed underneath Overlay, I added some yellow which transformed into more of a gold color and acted like a highlighter around the lightening bolt to help bring out its shape. In a grouped Multiply layer that I added to the top of the layer stack, I roughly outlined the edge of the bolt with a navy blue. Also in Multiply, I applied a black airbrush like mascara to his eyelashes along with a tiny amount of black eyeliner.

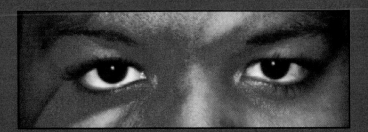

For the lipstick color I chose gold, which I achieved by painting yellow back in the Overlay layer – the highlights in his lips really brought a glossy shine to the texture. I also darkened the edges of his lips a little in the Multiply layer.

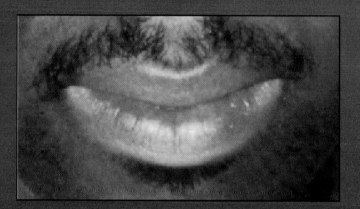 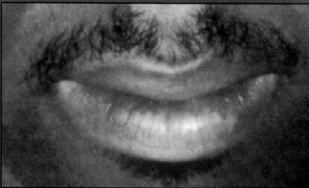

For this makeover, I didn't make a custom palette – the colors already existed on his face. I simply collected tones with the Eyedropper tool and altered them with the RGB Sliders. The main colors used in the makeover were red, purple, blue, yellow and white.

In a few short and simple steps, I was able to give Kymar a lightening bolt like on David Bowie's Aladdin Sane album cover. When the approach is this straightforward, the effects are just as enjoyable as spending hours crafting a finished portrait.

## Summary

Using these techniques, I was able to further explore my interest of airbrushed portraits. It was a new approach for me to address the makeover in a literal way, applying the Airbrush to the face like a mask. After I finished each makeover, I enjoyed hiding the photo layer to see how much paint I had applied to help assess how much of the portrait was actually made up.

On a white surface, most of the makeup looked like a colored pencil drawing or painting. Treating the face like a 3D canvas, Photoshop's Blending Modes helped me to focus on the photo and allowed me to be expressive while not straying too far from the level of realism that I wanted to maintain.

It's worth experimenting with Blending Modes when using a photo as the beginning point for a portrait. Personally, I'd like to push the approach I started with Barbara's glossy magazine makeover – experimenting with blur options and opacity to totally transform the photograph.

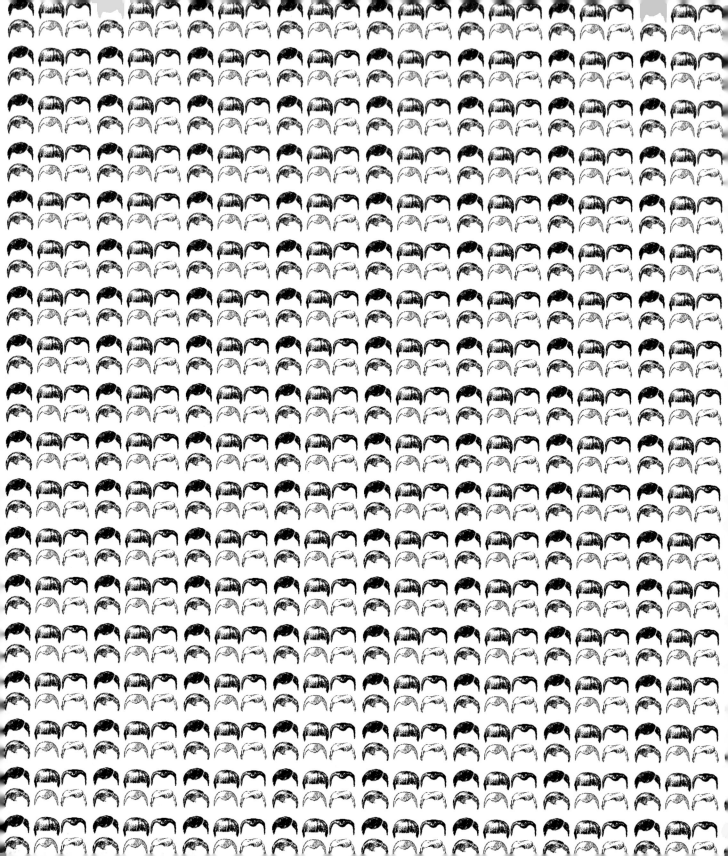

4 Art Mimicry

Let's get this straight. Many – if not all – lovers of art will find what follows offensive. It is disrespectful, dismissive, flippant and arrogant. But is it Art? For the sake of argument, let's say no. No, it's not Art – it's Photoshop. It's mimicry. It's helping us learn techniques we might not have picked up in past forays into the software by keeping our standards sky-high. It enables us to take inspiration and have the technical know-how to do something about it.

Don't feel bad. Artists have done it all along. They weren't just amazing from nothing, you know. All the Masters spent a good deal of their youthful years in apprenticeships.

So, whether this is disrespectful or unworthy, or whatever any art lovers out there might call it, we're going to have to learn to read paintings. We're going to break them down and figure out exactly what it is about that particular painting that makes it so identifiable. If we can get that sussed, it's just going to be a case of learning to do it in Photoshop. And it really is a piece of cake, as you'll see.

## Where to begin?

Have you ever wondered exactly how closely a person's portrait corresponds to their actual face? Of course it's harder to tell a lie these days but, in times before photography became a viable means of portraiture, perceptions of rich and famous people are tantalizingly distanced by artistic license.

After all, it's a popular slip-up to perceive, let's say Christ, as that popularly pale-skinned serene bearded fellow. Indeed, any attempt to suggest anything different is a positive wrench. A recent UK church-led advertising campaign depicting Christ in a suspiciously Che Guevara art-style was met with enormous anger from the more pastel-coloring aficionados.

Portraiture – and more particularly its distance from reality – is pretty powerful. So where exactly do we find the *real people*? Was Henry VIII really that *square*? Oliver Cromwell that *warty*? These subjects really do have a way of existing *between* the works of art that are said to depict them.

I'm going to take a look at this by using a single snapshot and attempting to give a convincing rendition of various artistic styles. We'll see how close they are! I used a snapshot taken in a kitchen with a single fluorescent tube for lighting, the night after a very heavy party. This will ensure the maximum wow quality from our Photoshoppery.

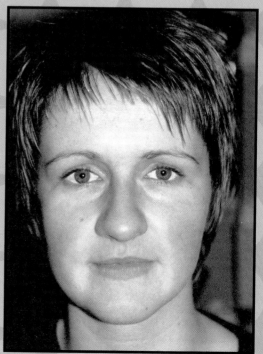

## Pop goes the easel

A good place to start is Pop Art. Those are some pretty imitable paintings. Andy Warhol and Roy Lichtenstein really did set out to make our lives easy. They've done half the job already by not really caring whether or not their work could be forged. It's not about excellence; it's all about image. So, seeing as we're not yet excellent, it's as good a place as any to start.

## Warhol

It's no coincidence Warhol is the easiest artist to mimic. He was all about convenience, which suits me down to the ground! It also means we're going to have to chuck subtlety out the window. We're on a production line here.

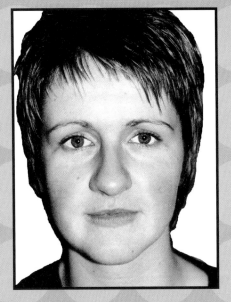

If you look at Warhol's *Marilyn* (1962), you'll see that the photograph used is of very bad quality, so that's the first thing we're going to have to mimic. It's black and white for a start – and I don't mean grayscale. BLACK or WHITE, like a jumped-up Rorschach inkblot test. To mimic the Marilyn picture, I'm only interested in the head and face, so I cut out all the background with the Lasso tool – just plain deleted it to white.

Next, I made a copy of the layer and used the **Image > Adjustment > Threshold...** menu option on the new layer to reduce everything to either black or white. However, here we get trouble. My picture is *so* badly taken that when I slide the Threshold level around I get either a great face or great hair, like so:

Luckily, we still have the original layer below. I then adjusted the top layer so that the hair looks about right, and erased the face area of that layer. Next, I switched to the original background and used the Threshold tool again to drag some of that subtlety back in (sorry, Mr. Warhol). Those of you with a more nervous disposition might consider adjustment layers and masking.

Strangely enough, it gives the image that Warhol-hair look. The rest was easy. I then flattened those layers and created a bunch of layers for each individual piece of the face. So, I lassoed around the lips and created a new layer following the **Layer > New > Layer Via Cut** menu option (CMD/CTRL+SHIFT+J).

I then colored it by pressing CMD/CTRL+U for the Hue/Saturation dialog box. With Colorize checked, I created whichever shade of lipstick I wanted. Generally, the Saturation has to be thrust way up to 100, seeing as Warhol didn't discriminate between shades of gray (or pink) too much. Reducing the Lightness also helps make those lips really potent.

Then I moved in to the eyelids, eyeballs, hair, face and background. And, I'm ashamed to say, that's about it. But using that technique, you can create as many variations as you like!

Both of these variations are based on Warhol's own colors. His classic *Marilyn* image used something based on human tones – pink skin, yellow hair and so-on. Later versions became a little more psychedelic, with even the black being replaced. You could try a few variations of your own, to see how random Warhol could get – or was he being very careful? You decide!

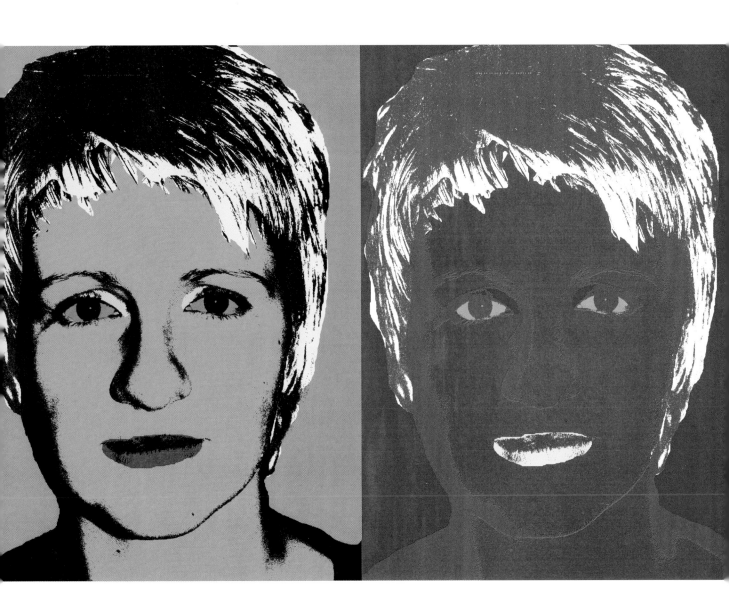

### Lichtenstein

So that was just too easy, and I don't feel like I've earned my fee yet. I tried explaining that I'm only contracted for 15 minutes of fame, but...

Let's move on to that other great icon of 1960s Pop, Roy Lichtenstein. Compared to Warhol, he seems a whole lot less cynical – there is craft to his art, so we can begin pushing the subtlety up a little bit.

Once again, the utter hopelessness of my photography was threatening to make this a difficult task, so I played around with the mid-tones in the Levels panel (CMD/CTRL+L) until I had quite a flat-colored image. Fortunately, it brought out some hair color to work with, while leaving those eyes still nicely defined.

At this point, I isolated the eyes so that I could manipulate them exactly how I wanted them to appear. Remember, it's all in the eyes with Lichtenstein. The eyes are the focal point (as with lots of art styles), and are often the most beautifully crafted part of a Lichtenstein print.

So, I drew a marquee around them and, as with Warhol, cut them on to a new layer (CMD/CTRL+SHIFT+J). From here, it was easier to work on them without having to worry about the rest of the picture.

For the time being, I simplified the eyes with a small paintbrush, making the whites all white (quite a task after such a heavy party), the blues all blue, and the blacks all black. Then, with a small-brush size on the eraser, I got rid of as much of the residual skin tone as possible.

### Aside: lines

Using this new eye-layer was actually very handy, because it allowed me to trace in all those thick black lines that Lichtenstein tends to use. Now, I don't know how far you've progressed in your Photoshop knowledge, but one of the most common stumbling blocks is drawing lines – simple lines. To draw a line, you need to use a guideline called a Path. It's rather like a bendy ruler. The mastery of Paths feels great. It feels like you've *arrived*. If you can use Paths, you can give any Photoshopper a run for their money. To my way of thinking, it's best to explain these things in full, because I'd hate anyone to remain in the dark about something so simple.

## Judging line size

Imagine you were drawing the line freehand, with the good old paintbrush. You'd want to pick a good brush-size, wouldn't you? So that's what we'll do. Have a dabble on the face with the paintbrush. Press CMD/CTRL-Z after every brush, so you don't commit anything to canvas. In this way we can choose exactly the sort of line we want to be drawing – how thick, how dark, what color, how hard and so on...

## Creating the path

Now, select the Pen tool. To create a Path, jab a single click at the place we want to start. Then we saunter over to the place we want the Path to finish. This time we click and hold the mouse button down. Dragging slowly away from that place, you will get one elastic line joining the start and finish points, and one pair of canoe oars. The way in which you drag these oars around determines the shape of your curve. So, drag the Path to a shape you want, and then stop dragging.

What you are left with is a Path curved exactly how you want. It's not a line on your picture yet – it's just a guide for where that line is going to go. Now, still with the Pen tool, right click anywhere on the canvas, and select Stroke Path. Select Brush from the drop-down menu, and click OK. Your perfect curve is drawn using the brush you earlier selected. Now press delete twice to get rid of your redundant Path, and you'll be left with the line you desired.

## Back to the main plot

On the Eye layer, I drew a series of paths to mark out the eyelashes, eyebrows, nose, lips, edges of the face and the neck.

Then I set about using the same technique to draw in the hair. This is the first place where artistic interpretation really comes into play. The hair has got to look good and comic book-like, so I simplified the fringe somewhat and began thinking about how I was going to shade everything.

Now of course, Lichtenstein doesn't do shade. Like Warhol, he's an Absolute Colors man. Moreover, he's an Absolute Primary Colors man. So, this hair is going to have to be flat yellow, and flat black. To this end, I started drawing Paths with the Pen tool in black, and then using the Paint Bucket tool to fill them with yellow highlights or black lowlights.

If you look at the image, the introduction of the yellow is a threshold in the Lichtenstein-ness of it. This is interesting, I think: At what point does an image become irretrievably the property of a given artist's style? This will become an issue with the artists I use later in the chapter.

Finally I ended up with some good looking hair, made up of yellow and black. To make this look better, I also filled in the background – one side white, the other black.

*Reverie* by Roy Lichtenstein
© Christie's Images/CORBIS

## Dots

Aside from the clarity of lines, the other main problem this artistic style throws up is how exactly to get the familiar Lichtenstein newsprint dots. As I've already stated, there is no room for shades in this picture, and we have to get the right kind of pink by using a very regular pattern of pure red dots. So what do we do?

Well, uniform dots are actually pretty easy to come by. Within the Paint Bucket tool, we have a Fill Option, which we can toggle between giving us a solid color or a patterned color. What we need to do is create a pattern of perfect dots. They've got to be the right size, and the right color.

My approach to this was similar to my approach for drawing lines. I played around with brush sizes until I had exactly the right size of dot for the picture. A lot of this is down to instinct – you've just got to be able to judge how red you want the picture to be, and how big the white gaps should appear. Prepare yourself for two or three attempts to get it right.

So, with my chosen brush size at the ready, I created a whole new file with a blank white canvas. In the middle of that canvas, I painted one red dot with my brush, and then I flattened and cropped the canvas, leaving a couple of pixels' worth of space at each side of the dot. I then turned the dot into a pattern through **Edit > Define Pattern**, and named it Lichtenstein. Then I closed my new canvas – there's no need to save it.

Back on my main image, I selected the whole facial area with the Magic Wand tool, and – note this – on a **new layer** I filled the area with the Paint Bucket. The Fill option on the Paint Bucket must of course be set to Pattern, and the Pattern drop-down must have our newly created Lichtenstein dot selected. Then I made sure the new layer was placed below the Eyes and Lines layer on the Layers palette. So long as this is the case, you should have something that pretty much resembles a completed Lichtenstein.

The only subtle change here is in the lips. What I've done is made the red dots white, and the white background red. It's a subtle change, but it does make the lips a darker tone of pink. I did this through lassoing the lips and then selecting a color range in there – namely, red. I painted all the red dots white, then inverted the selection, and painted the rest of it red. Job done!

## Final touches

So, how do we give it that authentic look? Well, the face as I originally had it looked a bit flat, and when it comes to highlighting, Lichtenstein goes for the dramatic. There wasn't a great deal of drama to the original image, so I made it up – lassoing a section of the skin and filling it with white. I made the eyes a bit bigger too, by just selecting them on their own layer and then using the Transform Scale tool to add those comic book proportions. A few extra paths found themselves getting drawn in, to bring out nose curves and eyelashes.

Finally, to stick to the true Lichtenstein primary color ethic, I selected all of the blue-green color of the eyes and filled it with blue dots, using exactly the same technique as I'd used to create the skin dots.

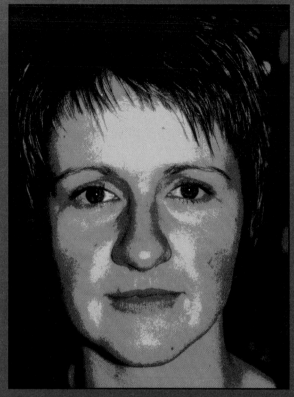

## Matisse

If we're looking to move on from Pop Art, then we're going to have to move backwards (historically speaking, of course). The challenges thrown up by an artistic style such as that employed by Matisse are significant. He uses more than just primary colors, for one. What is our palette going to be?

My way of deciding that is by a simple application of the **Image > Adjustment > Posterize** option. Taking the original photo, I posterized it – allowing for six levels of color. Here, then, are some good base colors to use. By these colors I will decide how similar or dissimilar my image is from a Matisse.

The next significant problem is that of brushstrokes. Let's begin by getting into Photoshop a bit. Obviously somewhere along the line, Adobe wanted you to think of it as something more than a photo manipulation program. We have Paint Daubs and Palette Knife among the 'Artistic' filters, so let's go for Palette Knife. I used a Stroke Size of 10, Stoke Detail of 3 and Softness of 5. I really want to smear those oils around:

So – at least we have some shadows to play with. It doesn't really give me a sense of thick dirty paint, but maybe that will come later. The next thing to do is get going with some brushwork.

The Matisse painting that formed my touchstone for this project was *Portrait with Green Streak* (1905), which has very unusual colors in well-defined facial areas.

Given the photograph I was working with, the color to choose for that central streak would be bright white, but I figured that wasn't Matisse enough. So, I chose a yellow and brushed it down the center of the face using a medium-sized soft brush at a fairly strong opacity. Then, using the dominant pink of the photograph, I brushed in the right-hand side, and then did the same on the left with a color that seemed to contrast interestingly. I also selected a brown from the hair and colored that in, before shading the face with a darker skin color. Finally, noting Matisse's heavy-duty eye painting, I selected a color close to black and painted in strong eyebrows, lashes and eyes.

So, Lichtenstein saw the face with blue eyes, Matisse with black. Go figure.

The resultant image is a combination of the colors that were in my photograph, and the colors that I expected to see from Matisse. It is, after all, his style we're after, and as we had to bend to Lichtenstein's use of primary colors, so we have to bend to Matisse's subdued hues.

*The Green Stripe* by Henri Matisse
© *Archivo Iconografico, S.A./CORBIS*

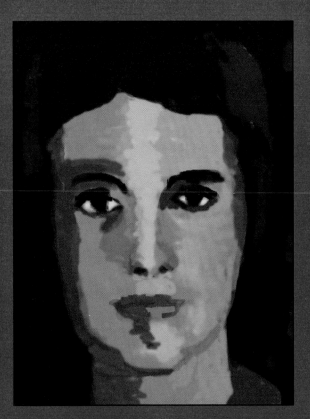

One of the very worthwhile residual features of conduct‹
experiments like this is a strengthening of one's reading of pai‹
ings. There was a reason for my painting the above version, a‹
that was I was 'doing a Matisse'. However: Does this look like t‹
artist's work? No. Why not? Well, because Matisse does not go‹
for strong contrasts in his colors. Darks and lights are in fact ve‹
similar. So, I toned them down by painting over them, and t‹
results are all the more pleasing. I also got rid of the dreadful da‹
background by copying the background of the Matisse picture.

Then, I committed what was fast becoming to feel like a bit of a s‹
– I utilized Photoshop – changing the Levels to make the painti‹
a bit brighter. In this case I slid the Levels arrow around until it re‹
something in the region of 0, 2.00, 200. It sure saved some ha‹
brushwork, and even Matisse wasn't that dingy.

One thing I found from doing that background was that the fa‹
was looking far too *clean*. So, I selected some colors that reflect‹
the Matisse picture I was working from, and painted in t‹
background with some experimental brush-shapes on the pai‹
brush. Chalk was pretty handy for some good effects, at a reduc‹
opacity of about 30%.

The background on this version is I think excellent, but tha‹
mostly because I utilized reduced opacity brushes over the top‹
other colors. Then it struck me: What am I missing in this pictur‹
Depth! Underpainting! There is a filter in Photoshop call‹
Underpainting, so I tried it. It didn't work, so I undid it.

The relatively time-consuming answer for me was to paint ba‹
over everything in a darker undercoat, and then paint *back* ov‹
everything in the original coat, with a reduced opacity. That had th‹
colors sorted out. You'll see I opted to introduce a gree‹
(eyedropped from the back of the original photograph). This wa‹
because I was feeling guilty about betraying the origin‹
photographs. Such things motivate me when I'm mimicking!

Finally, I added in a bit of dirt and grime in the shape of shadow‹
principally on the right-hand side of the canvas. This was don‹
again with a small Chalk-shaped paintbrush, set to black, but wit‹
an opacity of around 15%. Such things should be worked‹
carefully – in this case with a very Matisse-like jabbing brus‹
technique.

That's the point at which I chose to stop. I think that's a reasonab‹
Matisse rip-off!

## Modigliani

Modigliani was well up there on the stylization. The elongated faces on a good many of his portraits smack of African art, together with his fascination with reds and russets. There is an extra distance on the sliding scale between his work and reality. Figurative – yes, but iconographic too. It's a subtle balance.

As I said earlier, it's fascinating to tweak a picture and see exactly when it attains a recognizable quality of the artist in question. With Modigliani, first off I expanded the canvas. Then I elongated the picture with a square marquee and the Transform Scale tool, and it just looked like an elongated picture. You see them every day.

Then I selected the neck on its own with the Lasso tool and elongated the neck further, thrusting it out of proportion with the face. This left a bit of a hole in the middle of the neck, so I filled it in very roughly using the Clone Stamp tool. All staple Photoshop stuff up to now. Suddenly I found the Modigliani factor stirring. Then, carefully tracing the head with a lasso, and employing the Transform Rotate tool, I performed a trademark tilt of the head.

*Head of a Woman* by Amedeo Modigliani
© *Christie's Images/CORBIS*

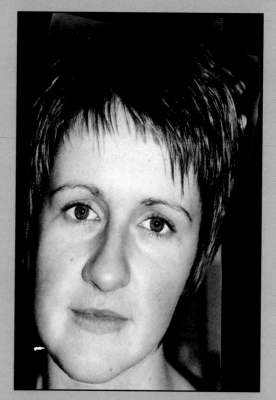

94

In a sense, that's it – job done. The rest is just going through the paces. Well, more or less.

Blocking the colors in is simple enough, with a Posterize, and then choosing the most apt color with the Eyedropper tool, before daubing the whole face with it. This time though, the need was for further elongation, so where I had a choice while painting over shadows, I went for long and thin. The nose is the most obvious instance where we can up the Modigliani.

As with Lichtenstein, this artist was very particular about eyes. Quite often in his paintings they are reduced to dark hollows, or even closed altogether. For a little variation on this portrait I've opted for the latter, thus giving that introspection that seems to suffuse a lot of his work. For the time being I did this by zooming in and carefully painting over the eyes with a small paintbrush. I left the eyelashes to mark where my shadows should go later on and then added a few daubs to shade the eyelids and give a rounded feel.

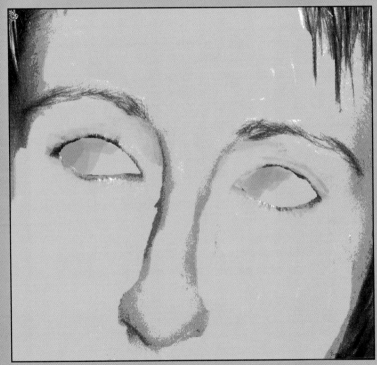

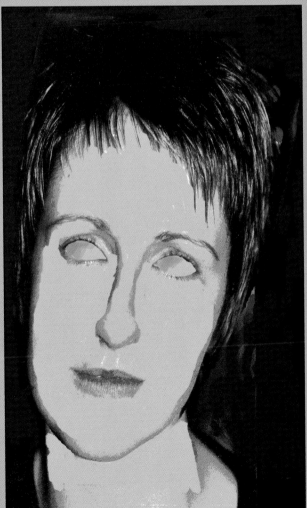

As with Matisse, Modigliani tended to keep shadow and shading fairly muted in his pictures, preferring instead to emphasize the fascinating shapes that go to make up his subjects. So, in this picture we're concentrating on the shape of the jaw, the neck, the nose, lips and eyes, while keeping shading and shadow to a minimum.

So, now for some heavy brushwork. Remember to keep those brushes quite small. I began the task of replacing that orangey shading around the periphery of the face (left over from the Posterize) with something more appropriate – a reduced opacity gray seemed to do the trick, particularly around the eyes.

The lips are important – Modigliani favored scarlet, pouting mouths, and to achieve this I used Paths (like before) to accurately emphasize the features of the lips that were already there. It resulted in a kind of caricature, with a really emphasized Cupid's bow. There's a running theme in Modigliani: there's a romance and sexuality about them, which is really emphasized by the lips and the faintly sensual poses. I told you we'd read pictures!

Next, I turned my attentions to the blacks. First off I stuck with the Pen tool and used black paths for the eyebrows – it's very important to get these right with one stroke (albeit with the aid of Undo...) otherwise our lady will not look as dainty as she should. I also put Paths in for the eyelids, before partially blotting them out with the Blur tool (from the Toolbar, as opposed to the filter) to lend a bit of subtlety.

Then I took the paintbrush and simplified the hairline into something much more reserved and 19th Century – something to counterbalance that brewing sexuality. You see, here I'm not mimicking Modigliani – I'm in his mindset! The hair I ended up with is a curious mixture of 21st century and 19th century styling. Pleasing!

I also attempted to incorporate some rosy looking cheeks. This proved to be rather tricky, so we'll come back to address this later.

## Filthying it up

Once again, a problem I encountered with this picture was the regular old digital problem – clean colors. Everything was bright and beautiful, and wholly un-Modigliani-like. So, in the Layers palette I created a Channel Mixer layer and played around with the colors until I had something a little more subdued.

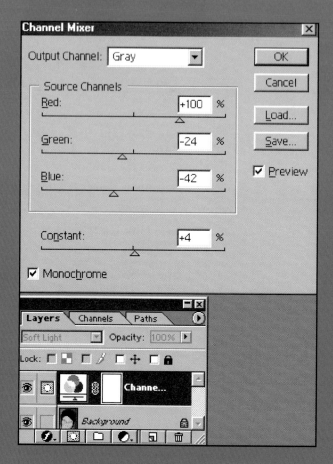

For the background I selected a color from the original photograph – there's a hint of green back there – and, using the lessons learned from the Matisse picture, began to work away with a reduced opacity and a tiny little brush until I had something I was pleased with. Actually, I think the blend of colors in this picture is exactly right.

Finally, and very importantly, we have a signature Modigliani style: rosy cheeks!

Now, you're going to have to trust me on this. I spent ages trying to get the rosy cheeks right. I tried soft brushes, pinks at 100%, reds at 10%, I tried marqueeing and changing the color balance and also tried the Burn tool. However, I just kept getting washed-out or circular cheeks or obviously shoehorned-in cheeks, or black cheeks.

The final answer for this subtle effect came from an unexpected source. It's a brush yes, but it's a weird brush. If you go to the brush shapes drop-down menu and click on the arrow in a circle to produce another drop-down menu, it can be found in the Faux Finish Brushes option, which you should append to your brush shapes menu. The brush I used is called the Mesh. It's really square and blocky, but it delivers exactly the right amount of color. I guess in a strange way it's the same as doing what Lichtenstein did – using uniform dots to get the right blend of color. Anyway, I chose a suitable pink, and this brush did the business for me:

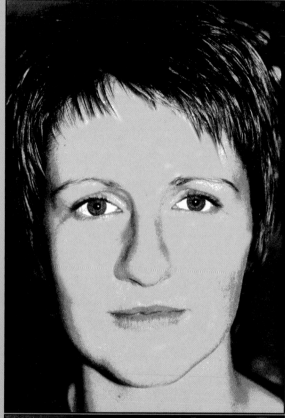

## Manga

The amazing thing about globalization in the latter half of the 20th century is that we can now get some amazing art from cultures that have previously been totally isolated from one another. The artists I've looked at up to now have been western Masters, but how will our face look with an Oriental look? Manga is probably the most exciting form of figurative art around, and it is the result of hundreds of years of Eastern thinking being twanged onto a Western pop culture. The result is some pretty amazing faces – so let's see how and why.

Manga is a cartoon format (note to self – one day you must work out what differentiates cartoon styles from non-cartoon styles) and so the face should be based on a single flat shade of pink. There are subtle shades to be added, but for a base color I posterized the face and chose one of the most pleasing pinks to paint over much of the face.

## Proportions

The first thing people said to me when I suggested doing a Manga remix of someone's face was, 'big eyes'. And they were dead right. The most notable thing about a Manga picture is eyes the size of saucers. In fact, the Manga face has proportions roughly equivalent to those of a baby or young child: Big eyes, small nose, and tiny mouth.

To capture the eyes, I hopped into the **Filter > Liquify** interface, and applied the Bloat tool to each eye. The real trick is making sure the tool is dead center on the eye, otherwise you could end up with some pretty warped looking eyes.

As I found, it's probably best not to let the subject of your picture walk in at this point. The result was pretty pleasing more or less straight away. That's where Photoshop's strength lays – excellent results in seconds. You've just got to know where to start!

Manga eyes can be seen as very beautiful or grotesque – it's a fine line. What I find amazing is that they're almost photo-realistic in a comic book world. I won't be doing anything to the pupils from now on. That's pretty amazing to me.

So, what's next? Well, as already noted, the background of this picture is hopeless. Really dark, and we're in a cartoon world, so I chose one of the greens that were just perceptible back there, and painted the background in with the Brush tool, making up any outlines I couldn't see. Then I turned my attentions to the other essential Manga feature: the small nose. Manga noses have no width to them at all. Like Michael Jackson's, it's all point. Actually, come to think of it – Michael Jackson's face is probably as close to a Manga face as you can get.

For the nose, I blotted out the bridge with my chosen shade of pink, and headed back to the Liquify interface. There I used the Pucker tool to reduce the size of the end of the nose, leaving it no width at all. Then I pressed OK to return to the main Photoshop interface.

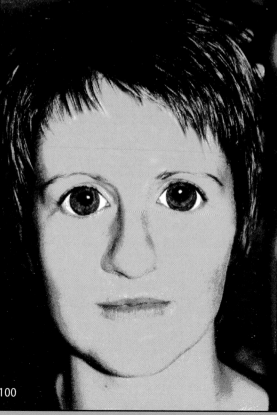

The final move to make in order to get the proportions right was to shrink the head. If you look, the head's just too adult-shaped. The nose-space is too long for a cutesy Manga face. So, I drew a marquee around the bottom half of the face, making sure I included the nose, and dragged the whole thing up until the facial proportions said Manga to me. Sure, the sides of the face don't fit now, but that's no problem. We have our proportions sorted.

Next, I turned my attention to the mouth, and this is where I feel that maybe my technique isn't as subtle as it could be. I slung a marquee around the corners of the mouth and dragged them into the center, slapping pink over any telltale holes left in my canvas. It seemed to work, though:

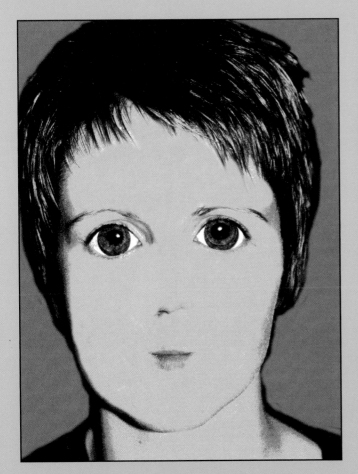

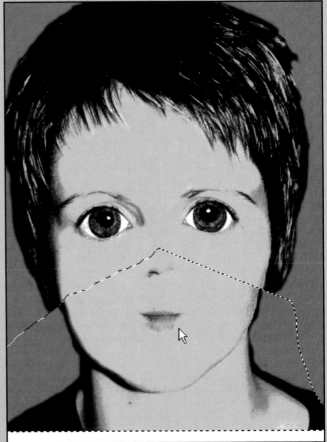

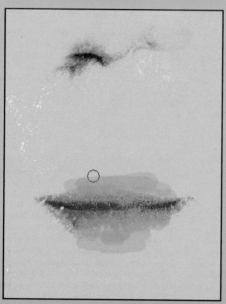

## Style

As I've said before, if you've got the proportions right, the rest is just style. So, what I earmarked to look for from now on is to get the final look of everything right. We've got to get the delicate shading right, get the expression of those features right, and for heaven's sake do something with that *hair*. Then we should be done.

First off, I reduced the lips somewhat with our trusty pink – using a smallish brush with about 50% opacity. I then chose another pink directly from the lips and painted them in a bit for that slightly vague watercolor look.

Next, on a new layer, I drew paths over the existing eyebrows, taking my color from the dark head hair. The reason I did this on a new layer was so that I could work on shading the eyelids without blotting them out.

To shade the eyelids, I selected some of the eyeshade that was already there and, using a 30% opacity brush, began to fill in. The nose sort of happened by accident from there – I just continued shading, and it was just *there*.

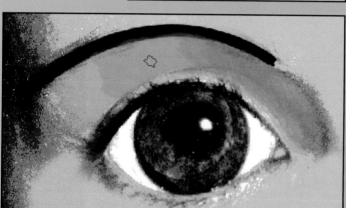

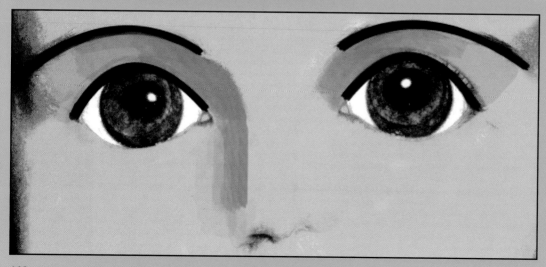

So, knowing a good thing when I saw it, I used that shade to fill in all of the other obviously shaded areas on the face.

With all the layers flattened, I began again with a new layer. What I wanted to do was sort out the jaw line. If you look at any Manga images, the profile of the face is really important, and picked out in black. So, using the Pen tool I traced over the shadowy jaw line I already had, and then on the layer beneath, pinked in any murky areas.

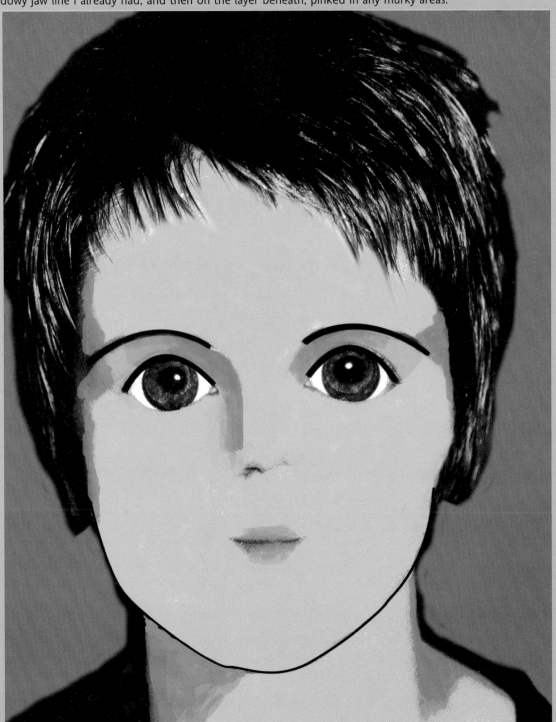

So – time to take care of the hair. Manga hair varies. Some of it is really wispy and time-intensive, and some is quite blocky and 2D, like vector graphics. I'm going for the latter, in order to achieve the maximum effect in the minimum time. As with the Lichtenstein image, I outlined the hair using black paths, and then filled it in using a flat black. For some reason, black works better with Manga hairdos – it's just more dramatic. Then I carved out a suitable looking area (using paths again) and filled it in a blonde shade, just to give the 'do a bit of shape. The addition of a white gleam added to the dramatic impact, and so I was encouraged to take out a bit of artistic license on the fringe, with a few spidery locks to blow dramatically in the Manga wind.

Actually, to tell you the truth, I played with this final image a little more, bringing the jaw-line up further, using the same technique as highlighted earlier. This final tweak gave the convincing Manga look; I hope you agree!

In carrying out this section, it's been interesting to see the different facets of personality that come out in a style portrait. For example, Lichtenstein's comic book style is the perfect method by which to portray a wide-eyed enthusiasm or fresh-faced youthfulness, whereas Matisse's method is much better at bringing out a pensive or glum quality. It makes one want to cast against type, so to speak: Do a really miserable Lichtenstein or a gleeful Munch, but that's another book...

Okay, so I think we've made the point about this one very badly taken photograph. Let's branch out and see how else Photoshop is going to springboard us towards the Masters.

## Van Gogh

One artist who's really going to put Photoshop to the test is Vincent Van Gogh. His paintings are full of vivid colors and rich textures. He painted landscapes, still life, people – anything. He produced a huge volume of work, but sold only two paintings before taking his own life. His brush strokes and paintings are full of the inner torment he felt throughout his turbulent life, and if you look carefully you can see his technique and his palette change and develop as his life progresses.

As you can see, one of the most important things to do is to give a bit of texture to the image. I did this to serve as the base onto which I could add paint strokes.

To do this I tried a new technique – using an angled strokes filter (**Filter > Brush Strokes > Angled Strokes**), using a Direction value of 50, Stroke length 15, and Sharpness 3.

OK, so we're narrowing the face down a bit so it's flat planes that are easier to work with. An art teacher told me once to think of the face and body as shapes as you would a tree or an apple. This is an excellent piece of advice because, as with Modigliani, it allows you to dissect the face more easily. If you can do this, you tend not to think about your preconceived idea of an eye, but looking more at its actual shape and form.

The face at the moment has too many planes of color. Rather than Posterizing as before, I decided to turn the image to index colors and give it 256 layers of color and then flip it back to RGB mode to carry on working on it. I did this by going to **Image > Mode**, changing it to Indexed Color, then again **Image > Mode > RGB**. This gives us a much flatter base to start the real work on.

I also wanted to make the background more like the Van Gogh self portrait above – this was his last self-portrait before he shot himself in the chest with a revolver, and his palette had become much calmer, and more toned down. So to change our background I selected only the background and using the Hue/Saturation dialog box, changed it so it was a greener blue in the hue, and turned the Saturation down so it was more subtle and less RGB.

*Self-Portrait (1889)* by Vincent van Gogh
© Gianni Dagli Orti/CORBIS

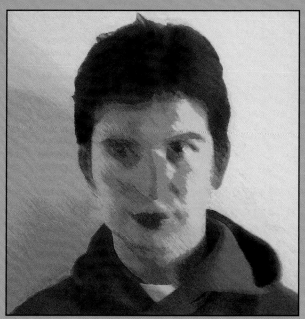

## Creating brushes

One major part of Van Gogh's work is his erratic brush stroke technique. The key to making the photo resemble a Van Gogh is to create custom brushes and patterns. First off I want to attack the background, for which I would like a fairly long brush stroke.

To begin creating a brush, I opened up a new canvas with a transparent background. As with the creation of the Lichtenstein dots, it doesn't really matter what size canvas – whatever suits you! On that canvas I drew using a small round brush, making a quick sloping movements diagonally left. Actually the smart thing to do would be to make two or three of them. Then, with the Rectangle Selection tool, I selected it and clicked through **Edit > Define Brush**. I named it vincent-bgbrush. Here's a selection of the brushes I made for this.

I decided to cut out the head from the main picture so I could make the background run behind it. I copied it and pasted it into a new layer.

The main thing I did was to try and imitate Van Gogh's fabulous swirls. To do this I built up layers of greens and blues and sludgy whites freehand, sometimes with a lower opacity to let other colors shine through. You see, I'm learning the trick about depth!

This was a bit too dark so in the Hue/Saturation dialog box I adjusted the lightness to +36, which gave a swimmy Van Gogh feel – something akin to his self portrait. My worry was that this just didn't have enough texture.

The next part I moved onto was the pullover. I created a new layer – and it was also time to create a new brush too. Looking at some Van Gogh portraits I can see that he used short stubby downward stroke for the clothes. So, I did the same thing as before – using a fresh canvas I made a new brush of short, stubby downstrokes. Moreover, I sampled the same brushstrokes and defined a pattern as well. This will save us a bit of time!

Back on the main canvas I used the Lasso to select the jumper. Then on the jumper layer, I used the Paint Bucket tool (selecting the newly-created pattern from the drop down menu) to fill it in. The problem with patterns is you have to create them in the color you want to use, so I had to create several. The first one I used was a mint-green. Then I used another pattern in a slightly darker green. This lends a totally uniform series of stubby strokes, so I offset this by using my stubby brush to mess things up a bit with deeper colors. I favored using the brush heavily where the material folds.

## Definition

Looking at a Van Gogh portrait, you'll see a deep cobalt blue (almost black) around the clothing. On a new layer, using a small round brush, I went around the outlines and folds of the pullover with a nice blue cover. I wasn't worried about making these lines perfect – in fact they look better the rougher they are. Imagine Van Gogh doing this with a thick brush loaded with oil paint – the pungent smell filling the room!

Looking at our face with its accented stroke I realized it should have slightly smoother blocks of color – not so pink but more Van Gogh-like. Yellow-ochre, vibrant greens, you know the sort of thing. I decided once again to shift the reality of the painting through the Hue/Saturation dialog.

I tweaked things so the master image was more saturated, together with the yellows and reds, leaving a weird greeny-pinky-yellowy face. Looks good to me! I also took the opportunity to apply a Gaussian Blur of 2.8 just to soften the colors up a bit.

Then I started with the hair and the face, making some new brushes some that were slightly shorter and matched the different contours of the face. On a new layer I started using the Eyedropper tool to select colors. Then I made them slightly darker, and applied them in patches to the different colored areas of the face. I found it easiest to apply the same blocks of color to similar tones so that the whole thing builds up together. When I'd finished this, I changed the blending mode of the layer to Soft Light in order to make the whole thing seep in together.

The last thing I did was to bring it all together by adding definition to certain parts of the face. Creating a new layer, I added strokes to the nose, neck and chin. Under the chin I decided to put a blue-ish line to provide a bit of shadow and to show the jaw line.

On the lips I added a less passionate color than the rosy smacker that had evolved. Looking back at Van Gogh's painting, his lips look as if they're already dead. The green and yellow are used to subtly flatten their effect.

### Klimt

What an excellent idea it would be to give your mother or grandmother a print of herself as an Gustav Klimt iconic lady! I'm telling you, it's a real winner! Don't you dare give me that vacant look next time her birthday comes around!

Gustav Klimt was an Austrian artist who worked at the turn of the 19th and 20th centuries, in Vienna. Much of his work is concerned with symbolism. The female form is a big motif in his work, representing death, purity, or love. Klimt's paintings of women are iconic works full of rich ornamentation, lush pattern and beautiful colors.

A huge part of his work is those glorious patterns, so I started off by looking at this. If you look at Klimt's most famous painting, *The Kiss*, you can see that the normally dominant female is surrendering herself to the male, in lust and love.

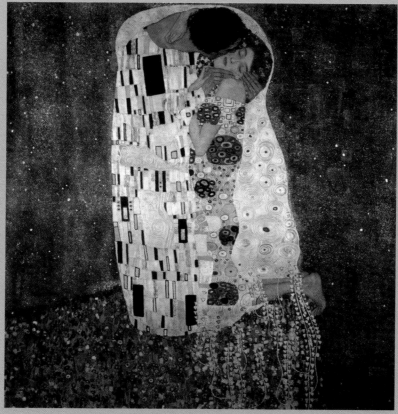

*The Kiss* by Gustav Klimt
© Austrian Archives; Österreichische Galerie, Vienna/CORBIS

The patterns here represent different things. On the woman's dress you have feminine circular shapes – they remind me of cells – which contrast with the man's tunic of angular masculine shapes in black and gold.

## Preparation

I took and scaled up the example from under the woman's right arm for my study (the greenish circle). First of all I put down a green background, with a large brush, with the Wet Edges box, on the Tool Options Bar, checked, and the opacity relatively low, just to gain a bit of texture. On a new layer I drew a rough sketch using a small paintbrush with a pale color of where my shapes should go. Notice how the shapes interact with each other, they kind of swim around the canvas. They are not all perfectly round, and they don't really overlap each other much. I think these particular shapes are based on anemones – they have the same colors as these flowers and the same voluptuous roundness.

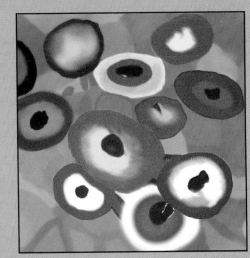

It's then a matter of filling them in. Klimt's palette for these flowers was deep reds and pinks with a hint of blue. The middles have white in them, but note that the whites are tinted with pink and orange, and even a bit of blue. This can make all the difference in whether an image looks right.

I chose to fill them in using brushes and layering colors of different opacities and then smudging it all together, but what you could do is draw lassos around the shapes and then use a radial gradient to fill in the shapes. You could put a couple over the top of each other at different opacities to gain a bit of depth. The final thing to examine at in the original painting is the background – we can see that the background is made up of different shades of green, in more triangular shapes. On a new layer I started to fill things in. And there we have it – one Klimt pattern!

## Klimting a photograph

Now on to the real thing!

The first thing I did was to deselect the background with the Lasso tool and quick mask so we are left with just the face and hair. I didn't create a perfect selection of the hair but I thought that would be ok because I would be painting over it later.

Then I put on a Smart Blur filter, so all the colors were smoothed out and the face was paler.

Now on to the background. I wanted to create a kind of gold background. Klimt's backgrounds look like they have a million stars in them, so I filled a new layer with a kind of yellow-ochrey color, and on top of that a more golden yellow with only 70% opacity. I also added one last layer of a dark brown which I set to Screen mode to give a subtle bit of darkness.

To create the star-like effect, I created a pattern, by opening up a new canvas, 1 x 1" square with a transparent background (here it's got a white background so you can see the dots) and just using a small round brush with slightly softened edges putting lots of dots on it. I used both small and large dots to get a nice starry feel, and then gave the whole thing a Gaussian Blur of about 2.8. Then, as before, I selected everything and clicked through **Edit > Define Pattern**.

Back on the main canvas, on a new layer, I used the paint bucket filled it in with the new pattern. I did this a couple of times on different layers, moving it slightly each time and altering its color in Hue/Saturation to build up a rich star field.

## Face style

Moving on to the face, the model is looking a little too smiley at the moment so I decided to close her eyes like we did with the Modigliani in order to make her slightly more angelic and dreamy.

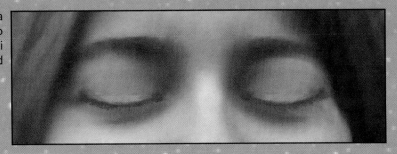

I decided that she needed to be slightly paler and more interesting, so I put the face opacity to 91%. To get the kind of blue tinge that you can see in Klimt's painting, I made a new layer and put a pale blue wash behind. This gave it a bit of depth but it was still not quite what I was looking for. So, I created one more layer, called foundation. I selected her face with the Lasso tool and the quickmask to tidy up the edges. Following that I painted layers of pale blue and peach, with a round paintbrush at 100% opacity, putting more blue around her nose and areas where there needed to be more definition, until I ended up with something like this:

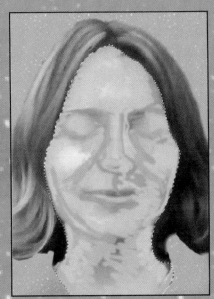

This looks like a bit of a mess and what I want is a rich foundation. To get that effect I feathered my Lasso 20 pixels so we wouldn't get any hard weird edges where the hairline ended. I then applied a Gaussian Blur.

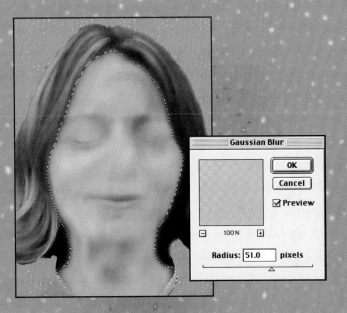

You end up with a blotchy face, which is quite like Klimts' faces if you look closely. You can see that they are not one smooth color but yellows, blues and peaches. I set this layer to 55% opacity in order to make it more subtle.

The Smart Blur I used a little while back gave the hair more of the definition that you can see in Klimt's paintings – strong lines of color – but the hair isn't the classic burnt umber Klimt favored. So let's make it like that – all we need to do is go onto a new layer, paint over the top of the original hair with a delicious orange color, on a low opacity. Once again we're going for depth. I set the whole layer to Multiply so it blended in with the original hair.

I created one more new layer called definition and, using a single pencil with a low opacity, I sketched a thin line across the nose. I chose some colors for the hair to make up the eyebrows with the same technique, and used a dull blueish-gray to shade under the chin.

The last thing for the face is to add some color to the cheeks and lips. If you look at the cheeks and lips in *The Kiss*, you'll see how rosy and flushed they are. This typifies Klimt's paintings. On a new layer called cheeks I drew in some pale peach colors and then painted on a darker pink then smudged this altogether using the Smudge tool. Then I set the layer to Overlay at 64% opacity, and there we have it – some rosy cheeks for our lady. The lips were created in a similar way, except I emphasized the Cupid's Bow, and changed the layer mode to Overlay and set the layer opacity to 86%.

## Patterns

Finally, I started adding the glorious patterns that typify Klimt's work.

I started to add some backgrounds for the patterns to lie on. Firstly a blue dress, that came from her shoulders. I did this by selecting the area I wanted it to go to, and filling it with a dark blue. Because this was a bit flat I added another layer and still in the same selection drew some roughly straight darker blue lines down it. Then using the filter Distort and Twirl I made them all kind of wavy.

I decided to do this by making brushes of different flowers and circles that I can see in Klimt's paintings, because I thought this would be the quickest and easiest way of creating patterns.

The ones I made are shown, left.

Using these I built up patterns in rich pinks, reds, blues and oranges throughout her hair and along her dress. I added in some hand drawn circles and smudged some bits of the blue dress together.

As you can see, it's just a question of building up as Klimt does, and thereby developing your own manner of symbolism and iconography!

**David Hockney**

One of my all-time favorite artists is David Hockney, a British born painter who lives in California. He was part of the Pop Art movement and paints the most wonderful vivid pictures and iconic visions of Californian life – the palm trees and swimming pools of the rich and fabulous. He also makes a lot of work using photography. If you haven't seen them you should check them out! There are two types of photomontages that Hockney makes, using thousands of photographs. I'll try to make something similar using one photograph and the amazing power of Photoshop... hurrah!

Here's the photo which we'll begin to deconstruct.

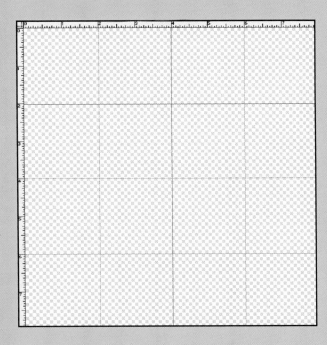

These images that Hockney makes are all about perspective and the way we look at things. To a certain extent they are a modern form of Cubism, which can be seen in Picasso and George Braque's work. Cubism was all to do with not just looking at an object straight on and painting exactly what you see, but trying to create the feeling of the entire object in a painting, by putting in the bottom, top sides and so on.

It's terribly simple really; the hard part is choosing your composition, seeing what fits and looks good together. I'm going to make a canvas 8 x 8", and within this canvas using the rulers drag out guides at two inch intervals horizontally and vertically, leaving something like this:

The first thing I did was create Polaroid frames so that I had something to work in. I did this by creating a new layer and, using the Line tool with a weight of 20 pixels, drawing lines along the guides, horizontally and vertically again. Then I switched off the guides:

Then I opened up the source photograph and pasted it into the canvas. I made mine a little larger before importing it, so that the focus is on Beni's face, not the space behind her. This also made the whole thing easier to work with. I put this new layer below the Polaroid frames.

So I had a grid and photo – now I had to start working with it. There are two obvious ways you can do this – by selecting areas, and cutting and pasting them, or by using layer masks to define areas of the image.

There is nothing wrong with using the old cut and paste method, but it tends to be a little more permanent than using masks. Masks allow you to show a selection of a layer, and shift it around if required later on.

With this in mind, I created 16 duplicates of the original photo layer (I left the original as it was throughout). I then used the Polaroid frame layer to select a pane on each layer, and added a layer mask.

This left me the same image as before, but with the ability to manipulate the layer and the layer masks individually. When working with the layer masks, I used a black Paint Bucket fill to allow total masking.

To imitate a Hockneyesque feel – one image composed of many images – I tweaked each pane a little, resizing, playing with the brightness and contrast, and moving them a little. I also applied a few filters here and there (but not too many), in particular the Blur filter – to blur certain parts of the image (imitating different focusing or f stops / apertures); and some lighting effects (to try and get that bizarre distribution of light that Polaroid images seem to absorb).

It's important before you think about what you are trying to achieve, what you are trying to say about the person (or animal!) you've chosen. It might sound obvious but certain personal features might be more expressive of the person than others, a little like a caricature, such as the hands of a pianist or the eyes of a photographer.

I think she still looks quite sweet, although it's a bit like looking through a fly's eye. The large example opposite is more focused on the glassy eyes and does look a little more expressive.

Have a go yourself, you could print the different panes on glossy paper and mount them on foam board and have an almost instant contemporary art work.

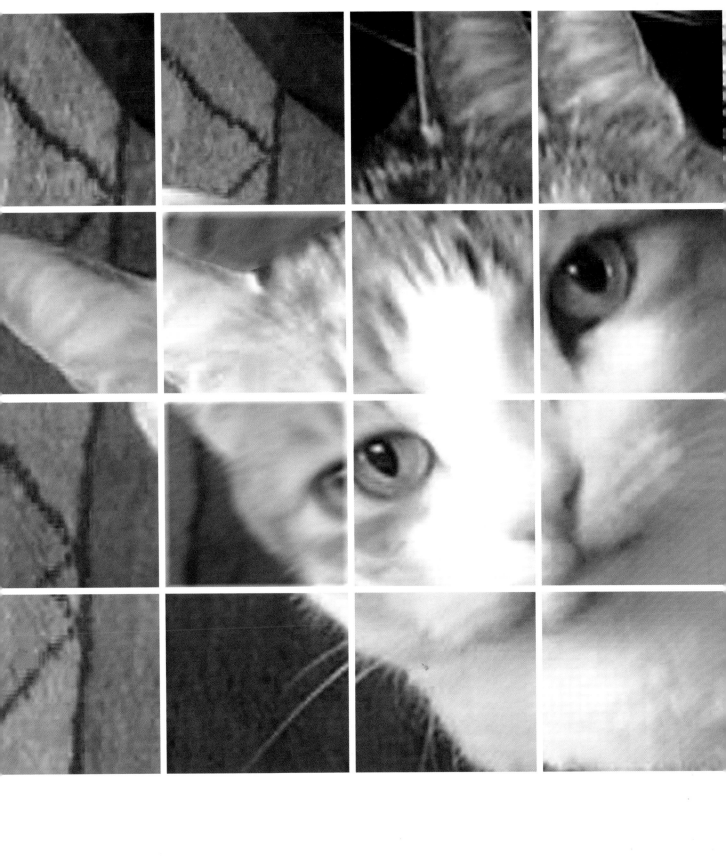

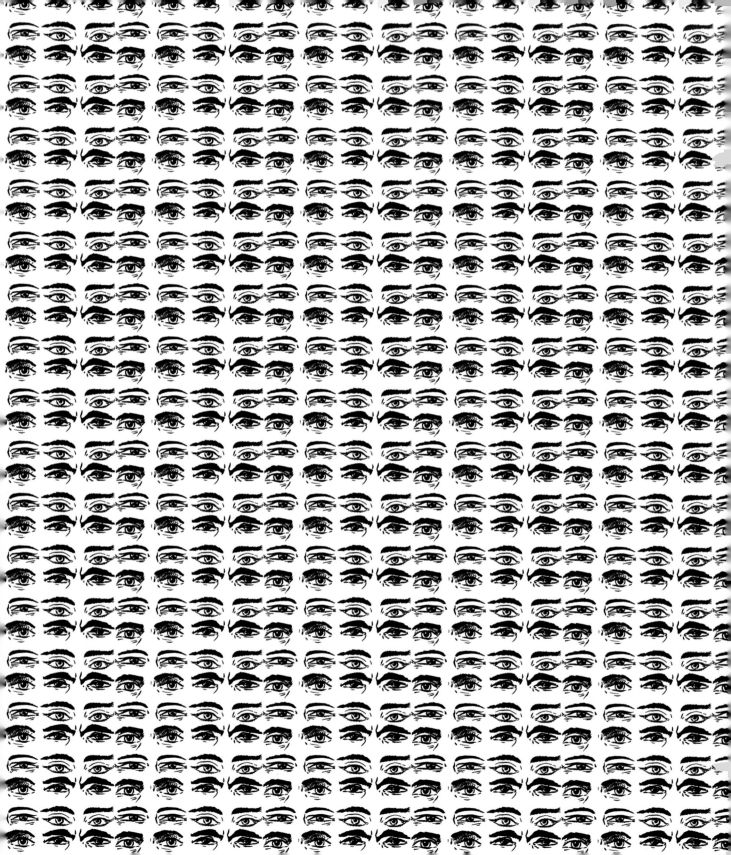

5 **Fantasy**

In this chapter, we'll be attempting to capture/convey elements of fantasy. Fantasy is a pretty abstract concept, so it's worth trying to understand a bit more about it to help generate some ideas for the images we'll be working with.

Fantasy can loosely be regarded as anything unreal or improbable, ranging from the supernatural to simply the highly fanciful. Fantasy is largely the domain of one's imagination and could be a sequence of mental images such as a daydream or a nightmarish encounter.

So, fantasy can be pretty much anything, be it abstract, concrete, bizarre or even ridiculously unbelievable. We'll attempt to incorporate these features into the images within this chapter, focusing on hellish/unholy entities and mythical beings.

Aside from the characters being fantastical, their environments should also reflect a fantasy element. To comply with a notion of 'real' fantasy, we'll also adjust the backgrounds of the images to help contribute towards the overall effect. We'd rather not confuse you by placing a fairy waving her magic wand outside a supermarket – that would make her seem as though she just escaped a mental institution, rather than being a mythical fairy.

Before we start, it's worth letting you know that James created the first five images in this chapter, and Nathan the remaining four. So, let's start jamming...

### Nalith – fairy

I knew from the initial brief that I wanted to make a magical fairy for one of my images, so I started thinking who I should cast this role to. It would be good if she already resembled a fairy – someone with features that could reinforce the transformation. So, my decision for using the subject in this piece was obvious. I gave her a distinct eye make up, styled her hair so that her ears were showing a little, and had her wear something white as this seemed to correspond with my vision of what a fairy might wear.

The photo was shot under a single spotlight with a system camera using regular film, and then drum scanned at a high resolution:

## Preparation

I made this image for our background, which was created by various 3D elements layered on top of each other using different blending modes such as Screen and Multiply.

I then put her on a new layer using the Filter > Extract menu option to take her out of her current background. This brings up the Extract window and we select what we want to extract using the Edge Highlighter tool. Mark the edges of the areas we want to retain with a little smoother extraction (5-10 on her hair, and 0-5 on her body). Use the Fill tool to fill the areas you want retained and preview it before pressing OK. (For those of you using an older version of Photoshop than 6 or 7, where the Extract tool isn't available — I suggest using Select > Color Range, or alternatively, the Lasso tool.)

## Retouching

The photo's poor quality and drum scanning has given us a bad lighting and ugly grain. If you look at the original photo, she appears not to have a chin because there isn't enough light to cast a sufficient shadow. I made a shadow by first making a selection underneath her chin using the Lasso tool with a feather value equivalent to the rest of the photo's edges (about 4), with Anti-aliased selected. The selection should cover about half of her neck so we have enough space on which to add shadows. I then created a new layer and selected a dark matching shadow color from a suitable area of her skin with the Eyedropper tool. I then selected the Brush tool with quite a large brush without hardness to its edges, and 10-30% opacity. I started brushing quite intensely near her chin, and eased off further down to create a realistic fade. Finally, I selected a Multiply blending mode to help the shadow I'd created blend more seamlessly with her skin, and then she had a chin.

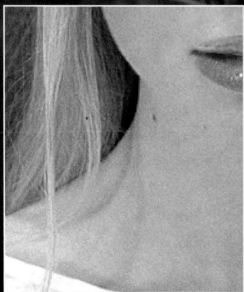

Before

After

The next step was to give her some supermodel skin like images in glossy magazines. Using the Clone Stamp and Healing Brush tools, I selected the areas of her skin that appeared more clean/smooth and applied these to the areas I wanted to improve. To add to that magazine quality, I created a new layer and brushed the areas where I wanted more contrast/shading – her cheekbones, neck and hair, before adding a Multiply blending mode (just as with the chin).

I then brightened up her face a little by doing some more brushing. I created a new layer, but this time I brushed with a brighter color, and added a Screen blending mode.

Finally, to give her that semi-shiny look, I first hid the background layer so the image became transparent. Next, I chose the **Select > All** and **Edit > Copy Merged** menu options, and pasted on top of everything before switching the background layer back on. On the new merged layer, I selected **Filter > Noise > Median** with a radius of about 8. Next, I applied a Soft Light blending mode and brought up the Hue/Saturation window (CTRL-U) to reduce the saturation to –60 so that it didn't look too color burned. Instead of using Levels to get the contrast I wanted, Median did a better job because it made her skin look even smoother, as you can see in the fourth screenshot below.

The four stages of facial retouching

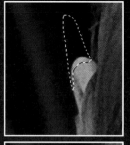

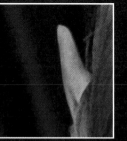

# Ears

I now turned my attention to her ears, and chose the Lasso tool to make a selection for her pixie-like new ear shape. I made sure the selection overlapped the real ear so I could make a nice blend between them.

I then created a new layer called Ear Fill, chose a color close to that of the existing ear and filled the selection.

I then copied a selection of skin from her face and pasted it on top of the ear fill as a new (grouped) layer and finally applied a Multiply blending mode.

I used the Dodge tool to make the ear look more realistic – brushing the edges for lighting or holding down ALT for shading to give it a more beveled look. Once I was happy with the ear's appearance, I merged the skin with the Ear Fill layer.

Fortunately, her other ear looks the same, so we can just copy the new ear extension and flip it horizontally before positioning it correctly.

# Wings

Before I started making the wings, I think I sat looking at the image for maybe an hour – planning on how to make fairy wings that are translucent, and of course how to make them look somewhat convincing. First I created a base and added several textures and translucency effects before simply duplicating what I'd created. When I had finished with the wings I was laughing a bit, because it was easier than I had imagined it to be. I can now make wings! I'm sure the techniques and approach that I took will be replicated in some way in my future projects. Let's roll...

# The base

The base was built up almost the same way as the extended ear – I made the selection for where I wanted the wing, and filled it with color (bright beige). The opacity should be 'fair(l)y' low so we can see through to the background.

In the same selection, but in a new layer I created a white linear gradient (white to transparent) that starts near her back and fades off about a third in on the wing. I gave the gradient a Soft Light blending mode so that the wing is brighter close to her body and becomes darker towards the top, helping make the wing look as if it is slightly pointing backwards into the image.

To add more strength to the wing, I selected the Edit > Stroke option with a Center Location on a few pixels to give the wing an outline. I then applied a Drop Shadow (Layer Style > Drop Shadow) with a fairly low opacity to enhance the outline a bit. This makes the wing look more contained and stronger for flying – even though we all know fairies fly using pure magical energy – their wings are just a distraction to prevent us finding out their secret!

## The texture

Creating the texture for the wing was a product of pure experimentation. I started off making a pattern with a thin brush, adding random diagonal lines all over the wing in a new layer. I then applied Filter > Distort > Wave to give the wing a more organic look and feel. You can see the lines here, before and after the filter has been applied:

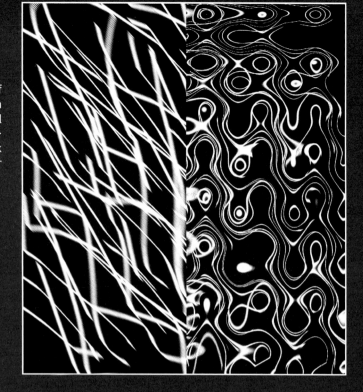

I kept the result of the texture inside the wing canvas and erased where required by CTRL-CLICKING the base layer (the shape of the wing) for its selection mask. Next, I chose the Select > Inverse menu option and deleted the texture that extended outside the wing shape canvas. Using Free Transform, I was able to make the selection fit where it didn't before (inside the wing shape), and I blended it in using Soft Light and Screen blending modes. I then duplicated the texture several times and gave each of them different opacity percentages and color hues, before putting them on different areas within the wing canvas.

### Inner lines: binding cell texture

This effect was achieved in a similar way to the previous texture, but I used the Pen tool to make random curvy paths all over the wing, before stroking them and applying the Wave filter again. (To stroke the path, switch to the Paths tab in the Layer palette, right-click and select Stroke Path..., before selecting your tool from the Stroke Path dialog box.)

The overall effect is less dramatic, but suits the wing rather well. I used an Overlay blending mode on this layer, which made it glow a little bit as well. Finally, I duplicated the layer, reduced its opacity to 75% and added a layer mask with a gradient similar to the one I made in the base. You'll see that the duplication glows a little bit extra in certain areas.

Adding translucency to the wings was easy - I simply CTRL-CLICKED the wing base layer to select it, before selecting the background layer and applying a Gaussian Blur (Filter > Blur > Gaussian Blur).

### Wing duplication

To duplicate the wings, link all the wing layers and put them into a Layer Set. From there, simply right-click the Layer Set icon and flip the new set horizontally. This type of duplication goes for the new type of wings as well.

commenced the final retouches by darkening the area behind her head to make it look less obvious that she had been pasted into the image. On top of the background layer, I created a new layer and added a black to transparent radial gradient so it covered the areas around her head. Next, on top of all the layers I created a new one and added another gradient in the bottom (linear and white to transparent) to give the sense that she's glowing a little bit out of pure magic.

I also decided to add a little more makeup, because it's popular among fairies to use glowing makeup that attracts more attention to the eyes. Using the Brush tool with no hardness and full opacity, I made a combination of dots next to her eye. Of course, I gave them a glowing appearance using an Overlay blending mode. I then put the additional makeup on the other eye by duplicating it and flipping it horizontally. I decided to put 40% opacity on the left-hand side and 30% opacity on the right, since her face is slightly darker on that side.

The image still felt a bit too bright, so I added Selective Color and Color Balance adjustment layers to help tone down the brightness in certain colors.

At this stage, I wanted to see a little bit more glow in the whole image. I merged the image into a new layer (**Select > All** then **Edit > Copy Merged** before pasting on top of the layer stack) and then applied a Diffuse Glow (Filter > Distort > Diffuse Glow) with a Graininess factor of 0, Glow Amount factor of 2, and Clear Amount factor of 6. Finally, I set the opacity for the layer to 15%.

## Focal depth

Up next is a nifty technique I use quite a lot, especially with photography. We're going to fake the depth perception a little bit by erasing Blur.

First, I duplicated our Diffuse Glow layer and then applied a Gaussian Blur with a factor of 9. Using the Eraser tool with a low opacity brush (about 20%), start erasing the areas in the image you want to keep sharp and in focus. Personally, I tend to use a fairly short focal depth because it makes the image more interesting. This helps to more easily emphasize where I want the view focused and which areas are more or less important.

I also wanted her eyes, and most of the face to look sharper. The upper wings are supposed to be pointing a bit backwards, so I didn't erase the Gaussian Blur further out on the wings because they are further into the image (less in focus). I divided the image into five depths:

> Foreground – for the glowing energy balls which we'll add in a moment
> Middleground – her face
> 1st set of wings
> 2nd set of wings
> Actual background – least focus

The final touch is to add some glowing magic balls, which will surround Nalith. They were simply achieved by distributing several white dots of varying sizes using the Brush tool in a new layer. I then applied an Outer Glow layer effect with a slight red tinge. And there we have the finished portrait:

I personally think it turned out pretty well. If I was to attempt this again, I don't think I'd do a portrait, but would put Nalith into some kind of magical forest environment. She'd probably be less prominent, but would still contribute a strong element of fantasy to the image.

### Délonia – siren

This portrait was a bit tricky because I started designing this image without fully knowing what it would turn out to be. I'm still unsure what she is, but that furry coat makes me think of a bird; I think she'd definitely pass as some sort of Siren.

This image uses the exact same camera as with Nalith in the previous example, but I used a stronger spotlight in her face.

### Retouching

To begin retouching the image, I pasted her onto a new layer with a white background. I wanted to use a rather bright background on this image, so masking it was a real chore because she's got a lot of swirling hair and the dark background digs deeply into it.

I started off using the **Filter > Extract** tools as I did with Nalith to remove the photograph's background. I used a big Edge Highlighter this time because she has a lot of hair with lots of difficult areas to mask. Once extracted, the result is pretty bad, so I have to do quite a lot by hand using the Lasso tool with a smooth feather value.

I start selecting the ugly areas and edges (containing grain and elements that were not extracted) with the Lasso tool, and then simply delete. I also use the Dodge tool to burn out her hair to blend with the white, making the edges less prominent. I also added a radial gradient to create a sense of depth in the image.

Usually when changing colors I add several adjustment layers. I don't follow a set process when I do this, but simply add lots of them, such as Selective Color and Color Balance, and change them until I'm happy with the result. Selective Color is among my favorites because it allows you to edit every main color and its inherent CMYK values, along with the white-, neutral- and black values. After applying Selective Color I wanted the reds, yellows and whites in particular to be changed. So, I took away the black (-100) in the red, and the yellow (-100) in the yellow before adjusting the whites to ease up some of the shine on her face.

Her skin doesn't need much retouching since the lighting was rather good from the beginning. However, I'll do some cloning with the Clone Stamp tool as I did with Nalith, applying the finer areas of her skin to where the less fine areas are. (That's not to say the areas below her eyes are *less fine* – she's beautiful – but I think they have a little bit too much smudged eyeliner there.) So, I lightened them up with the Clone Stamp tool using skin from her cheeks.

You'll also notice that now she doesn't have any shoulders. I deleted them with the Eraser tool, but was careful to go easy around the neck area to help create a nice tone.

## Fur Coat

The next step was to create her furry coat, which I started by making a selection for the base and then used the **Filter > Render > Clouds** menu option to get some texture.

133

I then colorized it to an appropriate pink to match her hair before brushing several fine strokes over the body to refine the texture some more:

Next, I copied pieces of her actual hair, which I resized, duplicated and then placed randomly over her body to create the fur. It's a good idea to distribute the pieces very randomly, and also flip or rotate them so it's less apparent that it was taken from her hair.

I then used the Eraser tool to remove any ugly edges that were copied across with the hair. These edges were rather dark on some sides, so I burned them a little using the Dodge tool again. It was also important here to put some hair behind her, so that she looked like she was actually wearing the fur.

For the background, I started by selecting the area I wanted to work with and filled it with a soft color. I then created a little texture, firstly with the **Filter > Render > Clouds** menu option, and then **Filter > Blur > Motion Blur** to help give it some movement. Next, I duplicated the layer, free transformed it with a little rotation and then applied a Screen blending mode, and then did the same again.

Now we have our texture, which we multiply onto our new area, and group them. To give the texture some more 3D feel, I applied the Wave filter again. You can see how the texture was developed here:

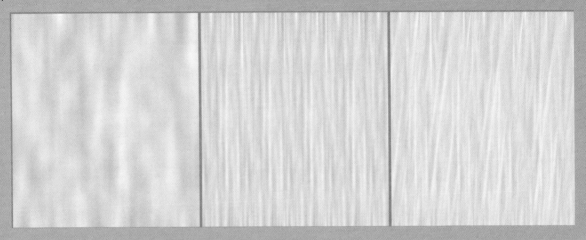

I then used the Brush tool to create highlights and shadows, which I then transformed into this:

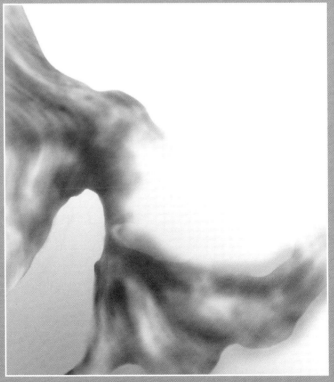

Finally, I duplicated the abstract using the Free Transform tool to make more original abstracts...

...and then repeated the same thing a few times:

Finally, with all the layers turned on, we have our finished piece:

Even though I had no clue what this would turn out to be I'm definitely happy with it. I'm still not totally sure what she is, but I think that's part of her appeal. This image was created in about two days, but if you have extra time it's often good to leave the image for a day or two, then open it again to see what can be improved or added. You often stare yourself blind – sort of like creating music when you think it sounds great, until someone else hears it and thinks it's terrible. When creating an image, I always try to factor into the process that I'm looking at it from an alternate perspective – as if it wasn't mine.

### Dakar – devilish drag queen

With this image, I wanted to create an ugly, devilish being. Having him start off making that really ugly face made it all so much easier, while his hair and clothes enforced the whole look.

I utilized the same techniques as with the two previous images – using the Clone Stamp tool to a large extent, and a lot of adjustment layers to colorize his skin. First, I made a selection to his face and body – going deep into his hair roots to cover that area as well, before applying Selective Color and Color Balance adjustment layers to the skin, and colorizing it. To make it smooth and to remove the sharp edges by his hair, we simply erase smoothly from his hair towards his face.

The rest is easy now that we've seen it in action with Nalith and Delonia. The most obvious changes are the ear, which we learned how to do with Nalith, and I removed his eyebrow using the Clone Stamp tool. I used **Edit > Copy Merged on** his Adam's apple and duplicated it before adding changes such as Free Transform for sizing and rotation. Creating the sharp teeth was achieved by using the Lasso tool to select areas where I anticipated the gaps would be. I then used the Eyedropper and Fill tools to select the dark color inside his mouth before using it to fill the gaps.

 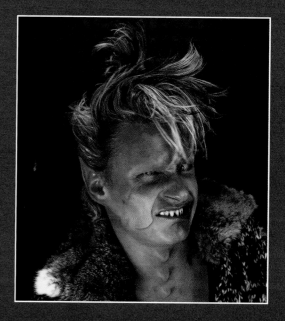

I think he does looks devilish – maybe not as devilish as I would have liked him to be, but he appears to be more fashionably mischievous rather than someone really evil who you would not like to deal with. I guess he should have had a more serious look from the beginning and taking the photo with a slight worm's eye view would make him look more powerful, but that's for next time...

the outcome – just pure experimentation from layer to layer.

Liquify filter and using the Warp tool, I could tweak my nose tip and make my eyebrow look a bit meaner. To pursue the look in my eyes I simply used the Dodge tool to burn out the colors – giving them a very cold and intense look. I manipulated the ear by...well, you know by now!

To alter the lighting, I ended up with many adjustment layers to get the look I wanted, since the original photo had pretty poor lighting. As you'll see in the screenshot of the Layer palette, it took a few layers for me to achieve the look I wanted:

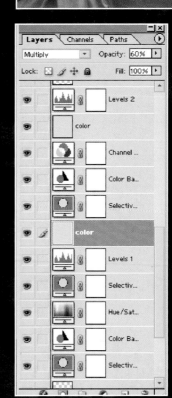

Next, I made myself look less inviting by flipping the image horizontally – for some reason, it just felt right. I once again applied **Filter > Distort > Sphere** over the entire image to make it inflate even more. The origin of the tattoo in my face comes from the photo of the reeds and dry grass below, which I pulled up the contrasts on using Levels and a Soft Light blending mode. Using the same photo, I duplicated, stretched, darkened and free transformed it to create the high grass surrounding me.

I then duplicated myself using the same approach as the wings on the Nalith example. I then pasted myself on the background and made small adjustments to create a little different character – my vampire brother.

The final stage was to create the sky and moon. I simply took a photo of the moon and applied the Outer Glow layer effect with a big radius around it. The clouds were made from simple random white airbrush strokes that I stretched with Free Transform, before applying the Color Dodge blending mode.

I like the result – the kind of style that I said I'd like to pursue with the Nalith image, incorporating more of an environment. I really wished that I had created more environments for the other images because they would have helped to convey the context even more: the characters would fit the theme, and vice versa.

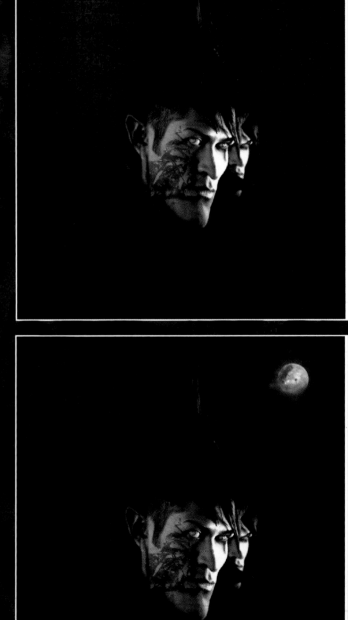

### Lothirade – evil witch

Lothirade is a remix of Nalith using simple edits to create a whole different character. There are no special techniques involved, so this will be relatively easy.

To begin I darkened the whole image using Levels. Next, I applied **Filter > Distort > Sphere** to her head, and to easily change the expressions in her face, I used the Warp tool in Filter > Liquify... to drag her eyebrows up, make her nose pointy, and give her mouth that sour look. Additionally, I filled her eyes with black.

Next, I selected her face using the Lasso tool with a feather value of 20 and pasted it into a new layer before applying the Screen blending mode. Using the Free Transform tool, I stretched the copy quite a bit towards the top right-hand corner to make it look as if it was her demonic soul flying out.

The reflected light streaks in her face are made of several white strokes from a brush that was color dodged in the blending modes.

Finally, I tweaked some of the colors with adjustment layers (only two of them this time); I removed quite a lot of saturation with Hue/Saturation, and gave it a greenish tinge with Selective Color.

That's how easy it sometimes when re-using material. For quite a simple process, I really like the result and would prefer not to meet Lothirade in real life.

## Dæva

For the next portrait, I wanted to give Megan horns and distort her features somewhat. My initial plan was to have her put sticks in her hair and create something from there, but I realized this wasn't necessary and I would be able to achieve a similar look as I manipulated the image.

First off, I retouched the photo. Although I wasn't totally sure how I wanted the final image to look, I was sure that I wanted it to look darker and less orange.

I modified the colors through the **Image > Adjustments > Color Balance** and **Image > Adjustments > Hue/Saturation** menu options and then used the Color Burn tool to remove her teeth.

weren't supposed to be there. Then, using the
Color Burn tool, I darkened certain areas to
help the eye modifications blend more seamlessly into the rest of the face.

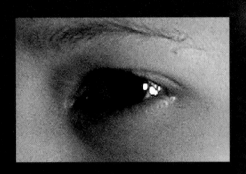

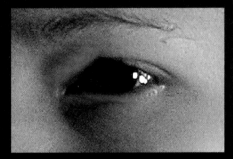

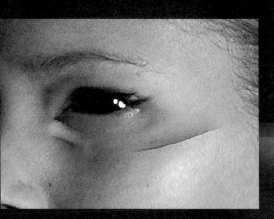

After staring for a while at the eye, I decided to start over and try something a little different. It didn't seem to fit right, so using the same techniques as before, I changed the look of the eye, by adding a scar effect. I felt this fit much better. Next, using the same technique, I 'embedded' a 'needle' into her face.

Turning my attention to the horns that I wanted to put on her head, I started out with the Marquee tool and drew the base shape of what I wanted the horn to look like. Then, using the Airbrush tool, I started brushing in some highlights, before adding some Noise through the **Filter > Noise > Add Noise** menu option. I then added some more highlights as well as darkening some other areas, using the Dodge tool. I also added a slight Craquelure to the horns through the **Filter > Texture > Craquelure** menu option. Reverting back to the Dodge and Airbrush tools, I continued to make small amendments to the lighting and coloring.

When I was happy with the result, I duplicated it, flipped it horizontally and then distorted it slightly using the Transform tool before scaling it down. Finally, I used the **Image > Adjustments > Hue/Saturation** menu option to make the horn darker by adjusting the Lightness setting.

Once I was happy with the look of the horn, it was time to make it look like it was coming out of the skin. Using the Clone Stamp tool, I grabbed some parts of the face and started painting some skin over the horn. Using the Burn and Dodge tools I shaded the skin. At this stage, I wasn't too concerned with the skin tone on the base of the horn, because I planned to adjust the skin tone in the whole image later on.

Next, I decided that her eyelashes should look more dramatic, so I painted some on using the Airbrush tool, and then adjusted the Color Balance a little more through the Image > Adjustments > Color Balance menu option.

It was now time to change the colors to give the image a more fantasy feel. Again using Color Balance, I changed the piece to a purple color, and added in a background containing a similar color. Reverting once again to the Airbrush and Dodge tools, I continued to add further elements of light and dark to her face.

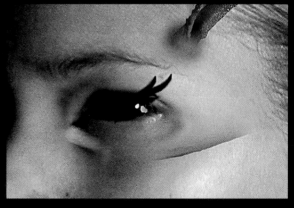

The only thing left to do at this point was to fix the area where the horn was coming out of her head. Using the Clone Stamp tool I added more skin around the base of the horn, before using the Dodge tool to darken the base of the horn.

The final image is shown opposite.

The development stage that probably took up most time on this image was the airbrushing. It's a time consuming process, but is always worth it in the end. Daeva looks slightly she-devilish, and I think that part of her face being shrouded in darkness helps to convey an air of mystery and magic about her persona.

## Bane

With this image I decided rather than limiting myself to a specific idea, I would work with the form of the photo and see what kind of hellish creation I could come up with.

Out of pure luck, his visible eye was white in this photo. I think it was the white eye that helped me decide to use this particular photo as it holds some good potential to create a hellish character from.

I set out by retouching the photo through the **Image > Adjustments > Color Balance** and Hue/Saturation menu options to create a base color that I wanted to work with. I also adjusted the lighting a little through the **Image > Adjustments > Levels** menu option.

Once I was happy with the colors in the portrait, it was time to decide exactly what changes I would make to the image. I initially planned on having some sort of beams coming from his eyes because he was looking up into the light. However, upon further observation, I realized that would be a little bit too 'light' for me, because I wanted all of my images to be dark in some sense to convey a disturbing sense of mystery. I started thinking of some video games that I've recently played or movies that I've recently watched, so I decided to seek inspiration from my movie collection.

I saw *Nightmare on Elm Street*, but it didn't really create any ideas, so I kept looking and came across Hellraiser. Perfect – I thought it would be interesting to see Dave's face full of needles. Of course – that was just the base idea – I didn't want to totally recreate Pinhead from Hellraiser, so I tried to think of a way I could connect this image to the previous one (Dæva).

As she looked like some kind of evil fairy/she-devil with dark magical powers, I worked on the basis that she'd cast a spell on Bane. So, rather than have Dave's face full of needles, I thought I'd make him look like he'd been turned to stone and skewered with some stone/metal spikes. Heh, heh – that's what happens when you disgruntle an evil fairy, I guess.

Interested in the appearance of how spikes going through objects might look, I stabbed some nails through a plastic coffee cup.

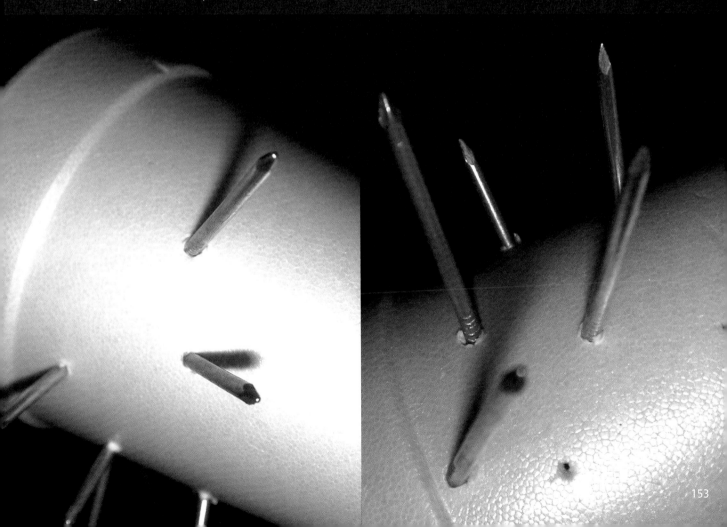

I was hoping that I could maybe incorporate these nails into my image somehow, but I don't think they would have integrated very well with this image, so I decided to just make the spikes from scratch. That's one of the things with Photoshop – almost everything you do is a matter of experimentation and although you will find them all enlightening, they won't always come out as you planned.

Before I started attacking him with evil spikes though, I wanted to add another disturbing element to the portrait, so I put some additional white emphasis coming out from the eye using the Airbrush tool.

I wanted the eye to have a somewhat darker metal, shiny feel. Initially I planned to apply this effect to the entire face, but I thought this might look like overkill, so I made his face look just a little stony and changed the colors slightly to match the tone of the eye.

So now it was time to attack him with some spikes. I made the spikes in a very simple manner, simply using the Marquee tool to drawing the basic shapes, and then roughing them up slightly using the Blur tool and finally erasing a little bit away. I made the spikes form in a way to make it look as though he was struck with them through his face in a downward manner – at least with the main (biggest) spike, anyway. I thought the composition of the spikes complemented his posture in the photo rather well.

So once he was nicely impaled on some spikes, the next step was to give the spikes some texture and color. Using the Clone Stamp tool, I grabbed a few parts of the photo and painted over the spike. Next, I spent some time using the Airbrush and Dodge tools and started shading and adding light to the spikes. This step requires patience – getting the direction of light correct can take a while.

using the Airbrush tool, but I wasn't overly concerned about how this affected the background because I planned to add another background later, which would somehow relate to the spikes. The figure below shows the change in lighting, and you'll notice that another spike was added to the top of his head as well.

At this point I figured it was time to begin the task of putting in the background, so I wandered around my apartment to see if I could find anything interesting or inspirational. I finally decided on a close up shot of an old style heater, which you can see here. The adjacent shot is after I have prepared the background shot to be incorporated with the portrait.

I began integrating the background with the portrait by placing the background on a layer above everything else, creating a mask layer, and then filling it completely with black, which erased all of the background. Next, using a small diameter Airbrush, I started going around the outline of Dave and bringing the background back in by painting white on the mask layer. This was a lengthy process requiring much patience but I chose it because I feel most comfortable with the Airbrush.

The next step was to fix the lighting of the background, and also to finish the lighting on the spikes. Using the Airbrush tool, I simply darkened or lightened appropriate areas of the spikes according to the apparent light source. I also blurred the appropriate parts of the image to give a better sense of depth.

At this point the image was almost complete, but I wanted to add just a few minor details, so I grabbed the Eyedropper tool, selected a bright color from the image and used the Line tool to make several 'strings' of light, and lowered the opacity in increments of about 20% for each line. I added a little extra definition to these additions with the Airbrush tool, and the image was finished. At the end both Dave, the victim, and I were pleased with this image. I had accomplished exactly what I was trying to do. The feelings I see emitting from this piece are failure, death, destruction, pain and isolation. Could have something to do with the music I was listening to!

## Unholy

The background for this piece is quite interesting, albeit a little disturbing. My original inspiration for this portrait is inspired from the movie *Fallen* where one scene sees the main character going through a book he finds in a basement. Inside the book are various insane and demonic looking beings and creatures and my first thought was to make the character in this portrait some sort of fallen angel. However, the dark around his eyes reminded me of a dream (well, nightmare) I had recently, so let me briefly elaborate upon my inspiration behind this image makeover...

The entity appeared in my nightmare with a sudden flash of light, before moving along the walls of a dark hall in a very liquid fashion – I'll be incorporating some blur/distortion to convey this. After another bright flash, I could see a close up of the being's face, with an evil looking insect creature in one of the eyes.

I know it's never the same when someone attempts to describe such personal events as dreams, but the being in my dream is the justification for this piece, so it's only right I divulge some minor details!

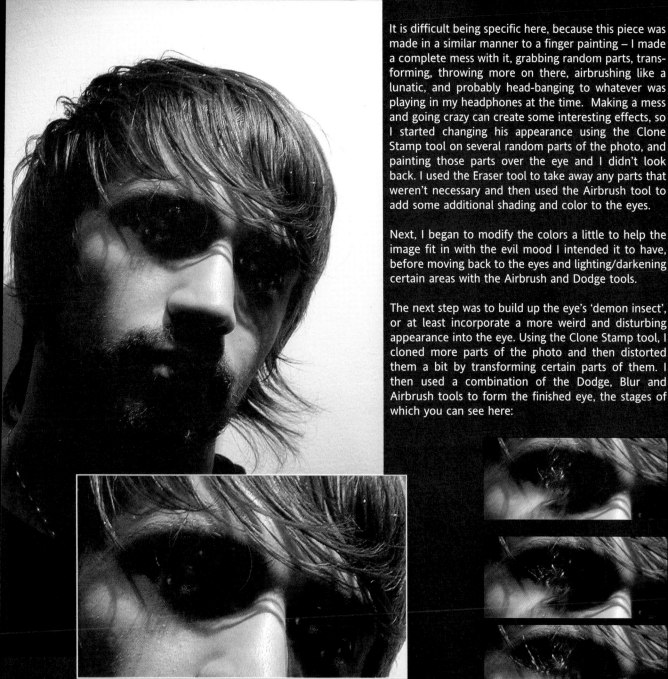

It is difficult being specific here, because this piece was made in a similar manner to a finger painting – I made a complete mess with it, grabbing random parts, transforming, throwing more on there, airbrushing like a lunatic, and probably head-banging to whatever was playing in my headphones at the time. Making a mess and going crazy can create some interesting effects, so I started changing his appearance using the Clone Stamp tool on several random parts of the photo, and painting those parts over the eye and I didn't look back. I used the Eraser tool to take away any parts that weren't necessary and then used the Airbrush tool to add some additional shading and color to the eyes.

Next, I began to modify the colors a little to help the image fit in with the evil mood I intended it to have, before moving back to the eyes and lighting/darkening certain areas with the Airbrush and Dodge tools.

The next step was to build up the eye's 'demon insect', or at least incorporate a more weird and disturbing appearance into the eye. Using the Clone Stamp tool, I cloned more parts of the photo and then distorted them a bit by transforming certain parts of them. I then used a combination of the Dodge, Blur and Airbrush tools to form the finished eye, the stages of which you can see here:

When I was happy with the eye, I reverted back to the lighting and decided to darken the image a bit. To achieve this, I Copy Merged the entire document, pasted on top, and then created a mask layer. I then set the layer to Multiply, selected the Airbrush tool and started painting black inside of the mask layer to take away the parts I didn't want to darken. I also lightened up his face a little and slightly modified the colors – mostly coloring the 'demon insect'. He's definitely looking a little on the sinister side, now.

I wasn't totally happy with the color of the eye at this stage, so I decided to modify the colors some more through the **Image > Adjustments > Color Balance** menu option, and also added some more lighting around the central part of his face. From here, I decided to create a background using the Airbrush tool. I also Copy Merged the whole piece, pasted on top, and then distorted it using the Transform tool. I then erased the parts I didn't like with the Eraser tool. Finally, I used the Blur tool to add a bit of depth and movement to the image.

Although I felt this piece was near completion, I still wasn't totally happy with the look and feel of the image – it didn't have the eerie sense of motion or distortion that I wanted. (Remember me saying that the character in my dream moved in a very liquid motion along a wall?) To remedy this, I used the Transform tools and the Airbrush tool, before darkening up the whole piece a little more.

To help contribute a little more to the sense of motion, I added a 'spirit' passing by very quickly. The "spirit" was created using the Airbrush tool, and dodging/burning in a few places.

That completes the image. The approach I took in the creation of this piece was very haphazard, although enjoyable. This image, like my previous ones rely heavily on subtle changes to lighting to help evoke a particular mood. Dark lighting really helps to convey a sinister sense of mystery. Hopefully, the elements of fantasy that I've tried to incorporate into these images prompt many questions about the characters within, rather than confirm any assumptions about them. After all, that's what fantasy is all about.

The model in this image loves zombies, loves zombie movies and probably is a zombie. It was obvious from the beginning to turn him into a zombie.

Matt was turned into a zombie using the same techniques as the other pieces – airbrushing, dodging/burning, and using the clone stamp tool.  The gash was started out with a bit of airbrushing, then adding some noise using the Noise filter, airbrushing some more, color/dodging... I expect you're getting the hang of my favorite tools by now!

It seemed like a good idea to show how one picture could go two different ways using the same basic zombie theme. If we consider the previous image to be a zombie from a movie – some sort of epic, shall we say – then it's only right we try to create a classic b-movie zombie. That's what I did here – deliberately making it look bad to give it a more authentic feel.

Basically, with Curves, Levels and Brightness/Contrast, I made "Zombie" as bright as possible, using a copy merged layer on top, and then using the Eraser tool I took out the parts that I wanted to remain dark.  Then I used the Airbrush tool and the Blur tool to fix up the piece and get it how I wanted.  After that I added some noise and reduced the quality to give it a more authentic feel of a b-movie zombie that is coming right at you to eat your face off, or whatever they do.

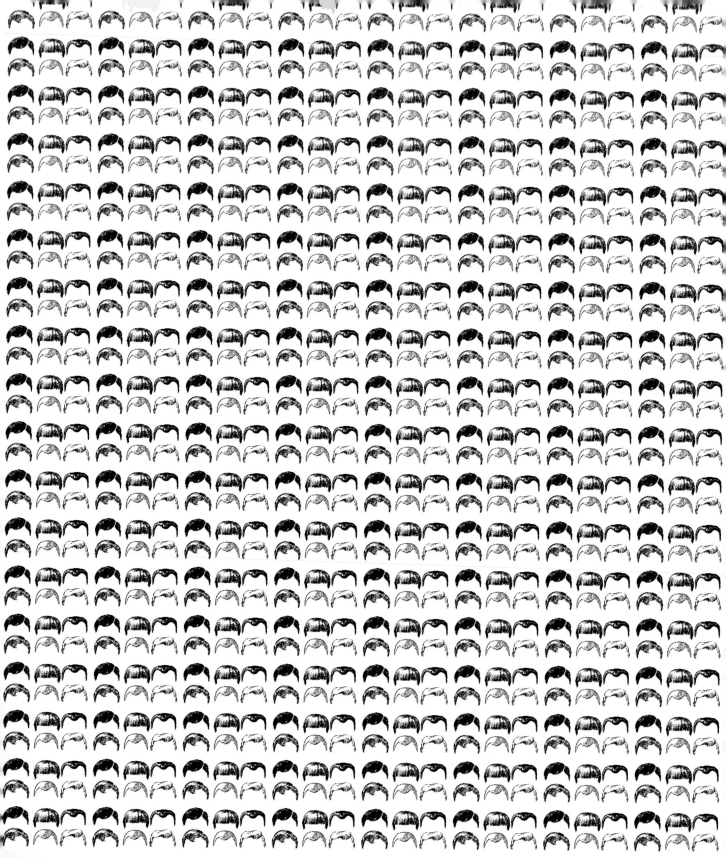

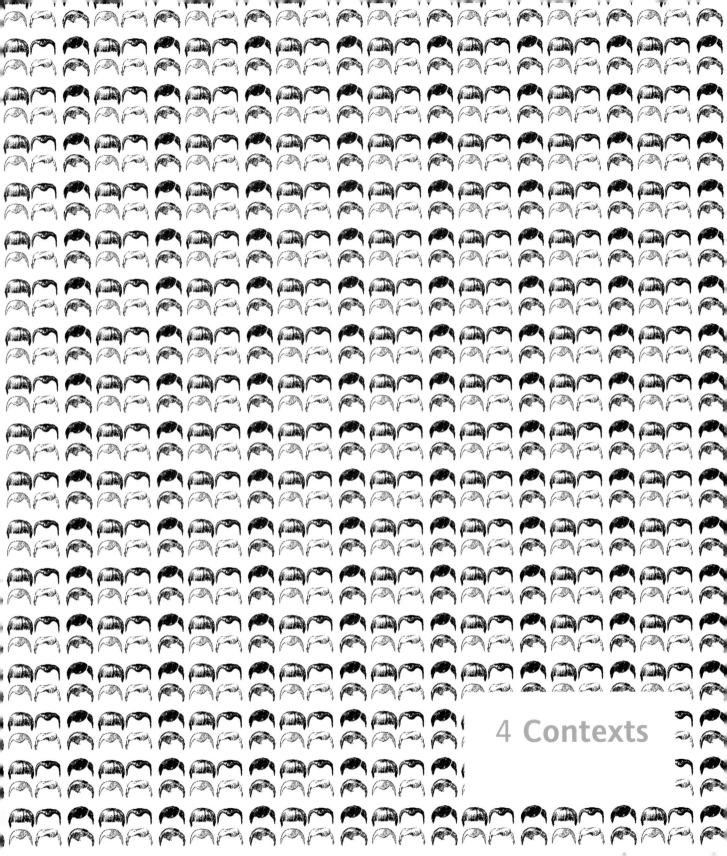

4 Contexts

When I started selecting images for this chapter, I found myself thinking back to those warm summer days from my childhood. Remembering running around the yard jumping in and out of the sprinkler heads as they danced from left to right in perfect harmony. It was as if there wasn't a care in the world. My only concern was where I going to score my next glass of cool lemonade.

Our eyes only met for a quick second, but all of this spawned from that moment, that tiny little moment. As I quickly looked away from nervousness I felt a sharp jolt throughout my body as tried to convince her that I was not paying her attention. As she turned the corner, her eye stayed clearly focused on mine. What was it? What was that feeling? Soon after my heart began to pump and race and I felt my body temperature raising. Soon after, she was gone. If only I had the courage to go after her and tell her how beautiful she was.

How perfect would it be to capture this moment in your work? We want love, anger, happiness and joy when we need it. And it's equally important to understand if you are communicating one or the other emotion when it's not wanted. Have you ever been in a working environment and you've been fixed on the same Photoshop canvas for hours, but it all seems blank to you? As soon as someone comes walking along it's a different story. They stop and tell you. "It's good" means t's just ok, but if you've really communicated your message they'll be impressed.

have been lucky enough to have worked with a handful of talented and aspiring young artists and illustrators. The successful ones can communicate their intended message. For instance, let's turn back to childhood for our subject; the old rusty can that you used to kick down the street as a kid. It would be difficult for us to simply render and paint a still life of the can and complete the story without some other metaphors relating it to our childhood, so by adding the element of a few old sneakers, and perhaps some jumpers for goalposts, we might begin to make that picture stand out. It's still a bit rough, so what if we threw a few running kids in there, struggling to be the first to kick the can? I think all of these elements combined could offer a stunning representation of that childhood memory.

This solution is all good because we are working from the ground up. First we found our subject matter, next we related that subject to a vision, and soon after we added a few elements to communicate the message. These techniques can be used by fine artists, illustrators, multi media artists and graphic designers alike. For a fine artist or illustrator they could render rough composition in Photoshop and transfer that to their working canvas. For multimedia artists and graphic designers our final canvas is the Photoshop document, so our results cannot be rough but must be clean without unintended errors and as lifelike as possible.

## Kris single profile image

t's important that I have control of the subject matter. I know from experience that it is very difficult to extract an object from an image if the background is very complex. So instead of photographing my models with a busy background I use a $10 drop cloth to eliminate the background. I'll go out and shoot the backgrounds at a later time when I have our model, Kris ready to go.

When working with this type of subject matter, you must be sure everything is perfect. If time is short, you only have the model for 30 minutes at $600 an hour, and your next model will be arriving in 7 minutes, you can see why this is a one shot deal. First be sure the environment that you are shooting in is controlled. A studio is best, of course, but because you are indoors you will need tungsten flood lamps with a high wattage to simulate natural sunlight. To avoid a synthetic feel, you could try shooting outdoors (but beware of the forecasted weather for you area!)

Look at a sample model in the area that you will be shooting. Pay attention to the darks, middle tones, and highlights of the person. Be sure that the lighting is diffused and not too hard. If the lighting is hard the cavities in the face may seem gaping. If the lighting is soft but steady, it will find its way into the small areas like folds and within the hair, which will make for a good photograph. Also, if the lighting is diffused and your shadow areas are not too dark and your highlights are not too bright, you can push it much further in Photoshop than you could with a dark or blown out image. There is nothing more important than working with good source imagery.

If your Art Director asks for you to work with bad imagery, be sure to let him or her know that the result is only going to be as good as the imagery supplied. We're often asked to work with crummy material and most times the budget of a proposed project does not allow $10,000 to be invested into good photography and models. So with this in mind, I'll work with one $10 white drop cloth purchased from Wal Mart, one $1.69 box of pins to hang the cloth from a wall, my trusty $300 S-10 Digital Elph from Canon, and a few very beautiful people.

As you can see in 1_kris_source.bmp the dark areas of the face can be made out. What we are looking for in a good photograph is an even tone from left to right in all areas from the shadow areas to the highlight areas. We can always add highlights and dark shadows later.

## Cutting him out

There are many different techniques that can be used to extract Kris from this background. I could have used a blue or green sheet in the background with even lighting, and in Photoshop I could have used the select color range feature. It is a good feature, but it does not give me the control I need over this subject. Because the pixel range of selection that I need will differ from the slope of the nose to the jaggedness of his hair to the crisp outline of his shirt, the color range might give me all kinds of different selection results. You could use the Magnetic Lasso tool in Photoshop, but the result in selection may vary. I'm looking for absolute results with smooth edges, and the ability to change that selection later. For this I use the Pen tool. It is a difficult tool to get the hang of, but once you understand how the points and anchors can be pushed and pulled, everything is production from then on.

If you're used to Adobe Illustrator, you should be right at home with this technique. If not, the trick is to click to draw lines between points, or click and drag to give your line a curve. It's easy after a while, but a bit tedious considering the detail involved. However on this background, where there isn't that much contrast, it is probably the most accurate method available to us.

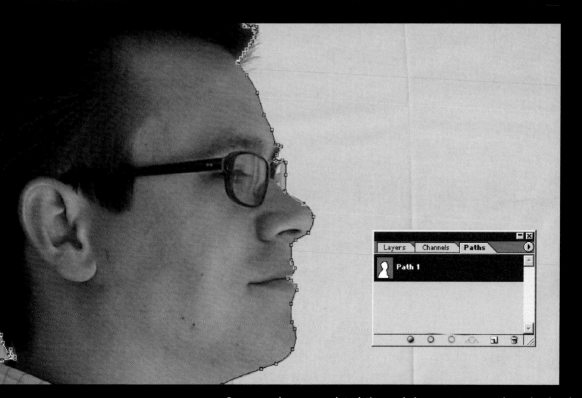

Once you have completed the path be sure to save the selection by double clicking on the path in the path palette, and naming it. This will ensure that your path will be available after you save and close this document as a Photoshop file. If you do not name the path in the path palette, the path work will be lost regardless of saving, so be sure to.

In the path palette, open the drop down features by selecting the black triangle in the upper right hand corner and select **Make Selection**. This will open a dialog box asking the Feather Radius of your selection. The minimum is .5 pixels which is acceptable; this will also ensure that your edges are not razor sharp. When your selection has been made, be sure you have highlighted the layer that you wish to extract the subject matter from, and copy the selection.

Next create a new document in Photoshop, with the background set to transparent, then paste in your copied image. This will create a new layer for that pasted image. At this point on the background layer I fill it white just to see if the image selection is going to work.

### A background

Now I need a background. I made sure that the lighting of the backgrounds was close to the lighting of the models, that being diffused and somewhat in shadow. If I chose to use a background in which the lighting were hard, I would have to make the lighting on the model sharp as well. It's not impossible, but why create more work for myself if it's not needed? Copy this background (**Select All** then **Edit > Copy**) and paste it in a new layer behind the Kris image.

Because Kris's hair is so complex, I have a little white left over from the past selection from the original path. You could use a plug in or a color range selection to extract the white color from the hair, but the edge quality might be lost. I prefer to leave it and modify the background to work for the subject, not against. It's a small obstacle to work around.

Also another problem is that the background image does not cover the entire canvas area in the background. Because Kris is covering a large portion of the image here, we can use a technique that will expand your image area. Make a selection with the Rectangular Marquee tool along the right side of the image. Next go to **Edit > Free Transform**. While holding shift, stretch the image to fit your canvas area. It's a technique that may save you from time to time when your imagery is working against you, though it clearly affects the proportions so only works on low detailed backgrounds.

Everything looks pretty good so far, but it looks as if Kris and the background are lit differently. To match the two images adjust the brightness and contrast (**Image > Adjust > Brightness/Contrast**) and adjust them to be as close as possible.

If you need to adjust the brightness or contrast of an image without editing the image itself you can do the following. While on the Kris layer, select the background with the Magic Wand tool. Stick with around a 1 to 2-pixel tolerance in the Magic Wand options palette. Next invert your selection (**Select > Inverse**). Set the foreground color to black, then fill your selected shape on a new layer (**Edit > Fill > Foreground Color**). You will have a perfect outline of the model with a 1-2 pixel tolerance around the edges. Be sure to have this layer above the Kris layer and set the effects to color burn. Lower the opacity to adjust the lighting effect you need.

### Shadow

Make a duplicate of this layer and set it to blur at 25 pixels. (**Filter > Blur > Gaussian Blur**). Lower the opacity and set this layer effect to multiply. Place this layer behind the Kris layer and move it according to the lighting in the photograph. The lighting here is important, look for the highlights and shadows in his shirt. You can see what direction the light is coming from. Move your shadow according to the information supplied by his shirt.

You can apply the same technique on a new layer above the background image to burn it too. Adjust the opacity of this layer to give you the match you need.

Everything is working fine. Just to round off that quickly-taken "reality" feel about the shot, I've used a few Gradient adjustment layers to create a Polaroid feel.

## Duncan's steps

Duncan has struck a dramatic pose, he is clearly lower to the ground than Kris was, so I knew that I would have to kneel while shooting the background, too. One of the advantages of the white cloth is that it helps give a bit of reflected light in the shadows, so we can still make out the information that is in the shadow area, giving an ambient light feel – handy for many alternative backgrounds.

Again, we're concentrating on control of the image and results here. You could use the Color Range tool, but I have decided not to because of the uncontrollable selection result when using the color range selector. (You can access it using **Select > Color Range**, and it is effective when used against clearly-lit blue-screen or green-screen backgrounds)

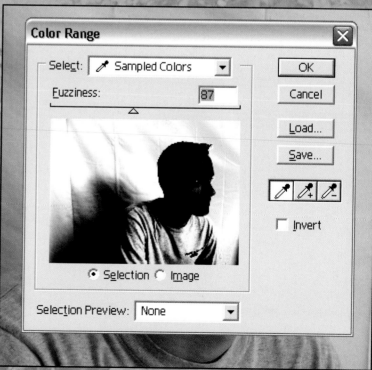

To get the results I need, I have decided to use the Pen tool, as before, and feather the resulting selection by the same 0.5 value. You can feather the selection further later, but for now you want a clean edge, but not super sharp.

Go to **Edit > Copy** and create your new document. In this new document go to **Edit > Paste**. This will create a new layer with the Duncan image on it. This is where it helps if you've been working at the same resolution all along. For the most part, a composite image can only be as good as lowest resolution component. The exception to that rule is in a situation where you will be slightly blurring a layer to give a depth of field effect, but even then it is better to start at a high resolution.

Now that I have a new document set up with my foreground imagery in place, it's all essentially downhill from here. Next, let's setup a background image for Duncan. We need a low to the ground type of image because I have Duncan crouched down for this shot. Here I have shot an image that I feel would fit him perfectly. A good tip is to photograph your models first, print them out on a good paper, then take the photos out in the field as you are photographing your backgrounds. This meant that the search for backgrounds took only a couple of hours, as I could be sure about suitability there and then.

In this case, I realize that the lighting and angle seem opposite to Duncan's pose. No problem – I flipped the background image to match Duncan in the new canvas. In order to do this I open the background image separate from the new canvas that we created for Duncan, and dragged and dropped the image using the black Move tool. After I rearranged the layers (placing the background below Duncan) I selected the background layer and went to **Edit > Transform > Flip Horizontal**. This made the lighting work perfectly.

As soon as you have both images together, be sure to adjust the brightness and contrast by going to **Image > Adjust > Brightness/Contrast** on each image. The source images may be a bit too bright or dark for that matter to work with raw. So feel free to modify the contrast to your liking. Also while we're on the subject, be sure that your images are fairly bright if you're going to print. If the images are too dark, the final print may be close to black.

It actually looks as though Duncan is sitting on the steps. Next let's adjust the lighting in both images to find a happy medium.

Using the Layers palette, drag the Duncan layer to the New Layer icon at the bottom. With your new layer selected, move the **Image > Adjustments > Brightness/Contrast** sliders to the far left (-100 each), turning your new layer completely black. You could also apply a blur to soften the edges very slightly if you wish.

Use the layer effects on this layer to Color Burn. This will adjust the contrast of the image below this layer, that which happens to be Duncan. If you wish, you could make a duplicate of this layer by going to **Layer > Duplicate Layer** and inverting the color from black to white. Set the effect on this layer from color burn to color dodge and see what happens. The colors below will begin to white out, adjust the opacity of this layer to match your needs.

Then try the same technique on the background. This should place the lighting of the two images in the same ballpark of realism. I think considering they were shot about 20 miles apart that we're doing pretty well thus far.

Now that the images are adjusted to look lifelike, I want to give the canvases a special touch. I mentioned before that I was looking for a Polaroid type of output. The more and more that I think about it, it just feels like summer. I guess that, because the summer is coming around as I write, I'm just in that kind of mood.

I am going to make a few more layers and fill them with warm colors. One of the layers has a warm red gradient as you can see. Next I set each layer to soft light in the effects palette for each layer. I lower the opacity to the feel I want and then proceed to desaturate the images. By desaturating the images I can get the warm hue from the color burn layers above, but take out any cool colors. I just want to make the canvas feel like a warm summer day. Also, this is what it looks like here in Laguna Beach CA, where I live during the summer. It's so cool.

If you want to give your images a bit of a glow, try this technique. Take the image layer and duplicate it. Next take that layer and go to **Effect > Blur > Gaussian Blur** and set the blue in the pop-up to 5 pixels. Lower the opacity of that layer to somewhere in the neighbourhood of 20%-30%. With this technique you retain the sharpness of the image in the background but also retain the soft glow from the Gaussian blur image in the foreground. It's also a pretty good technique to use if you have to work with a bad scan or if your image quality is poor.

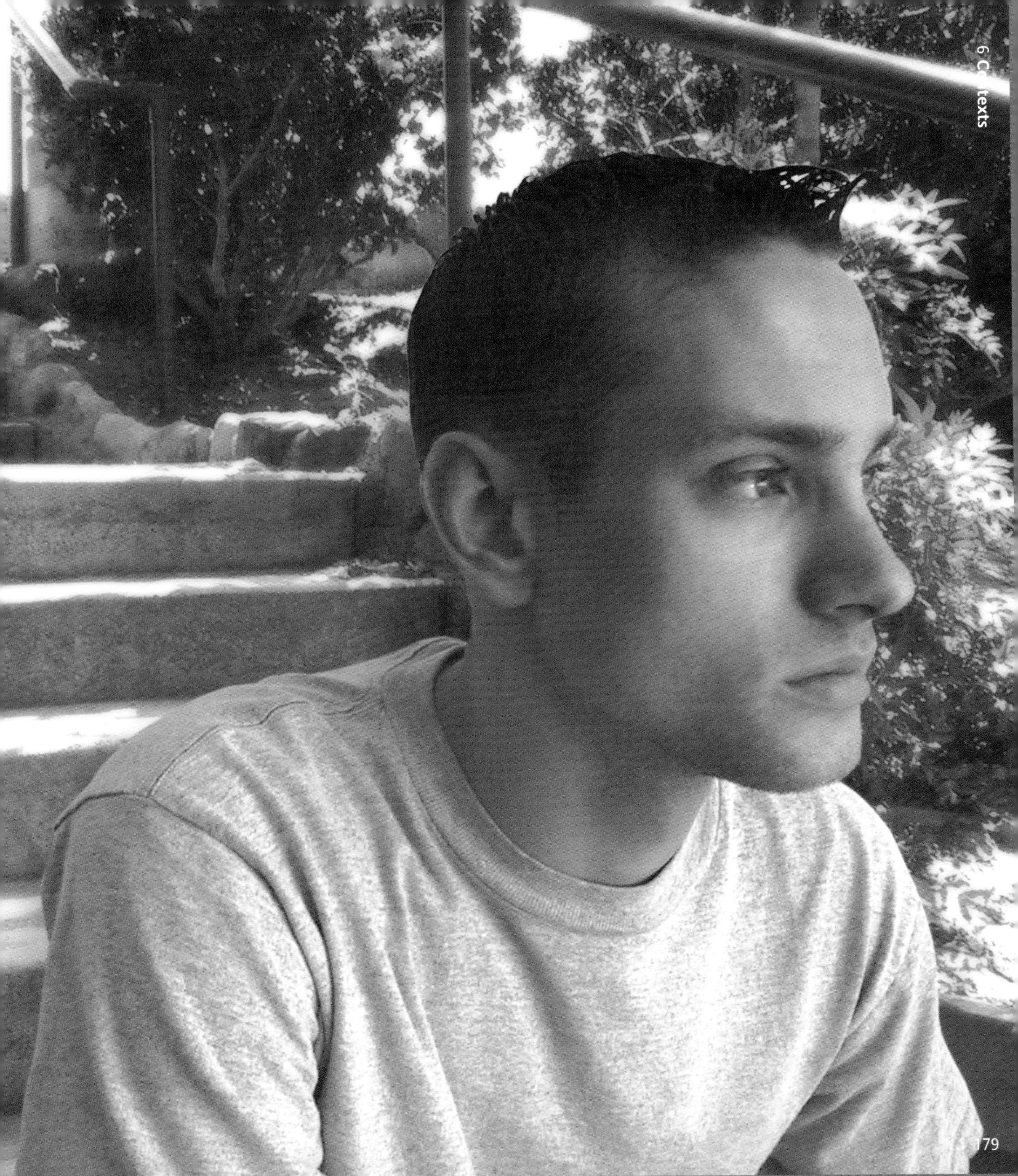

# Derek

A few fine artists have told me that the most difficult models to work with are children. This doesn't have anything to do with psyche, but instead deals with the plush skin and distorted body composition of young people. As you can see Derek's head in proportion to his body is extreme. In order to make this static image come to life, I had to photograph him from an angle that was not too high above his head. If I were from a bird's eye perspective looking down on Derek, all I would see is his head. And likewise if I were to photograph him from a worm's eye perspective, the proportions would be way off, especially after the synthetic distortion that a lens adds to the melting pot. What I have learned from photographing children is that if you kneel a bit, their bodies don't look so distorted. I'm sure you'll run into the same type of issues if you ever have to document young children for your work.

Take a look at the original image I have here of Derek. He has a few curls of hair coming out of the top left side of his head. This with the pen tool can be difficult to capture without keeping some of the white background. So instead, I have decided to run my path right through it.

Let's find a good background to suit this foreground image. Here's a fun and curious image. I think it matches that devilish look on Derek's face. Believe me (he's my son), he can be a rascal and this tree is a hidden oasis of fun. The image is good but I can already see an issue with it. The lighting is pretty sharp. In the back the shadows are fine, but look at those hard white areas where the light shines through the branches. Luckily, it looks as if we're in the shade, so I won't have to apply any bright spots to Derek's image to give the appearance that he is half in light, half in shadow.

Next take your background image and drag and drop it from its canvas to the new canvas that we created for Derek. Rearrange the layer so that the background image is below the Derek image. As you can already see, Derek is much lighter than the background image. I could do a few things here. I could use the brightness and contrast feature to make Derek a bit darker. Or, I could proceed in creating a new layer above Derek with a black and setting the layer effect to color burn. This would give me the effect I want to help match the lighting of Derek to the background. Let's do both to make it work.

On the Derek layer use the magic wand tool to create a selection in the transparent areas around Derek. Now go to **Select > Inverse** again to get a perfect selection of Derek, then feather with a radius of about 3 pixels. This will make sure that when you apply the color burn or color dodge feature on a layer on top of the Derek layer you will not get a sharp edge around him. That might give that cookie cutter type of look that we want to be sure to avoid. Once you have your selection ready, fill it with black on a new layer as seen above and set the layer effect to color burn. Lower the opacity of the layer until your desired look is achieved with the Derek image below.

Now that I have Derek working better with the background, I have decided to adjust the background layer as well. To do this I have made a new layer above the background layer and have filled it entirely with black. Next I lowered the opacity to match the same overall tone of Derek. When I felt comfortable with the results I move on to stylizing the canvas with my Polaroid Summertime effect.

Finally, you can create that nostalgic look by taking a duplicate of the background layer, applying a Gaussian Blur filter and lowering the opacity to suit you. You could apply this to the whole image, but by just treating the background we retain the sharpness of the face and eyes. An alternative would be to treat any areas you especially want to pick out manually later with the eraser.

Opposite is the image with the background and Derek both desaturated by going to **Image > Adjust > Hue/Saturation**. I did not desaturate the images fully, but if I did the soft light layers would bring that warm skin tone back to the imagery. The most important information in the imagery is the gradients from dark to light. If you have those you can apply any color to your subjects.

## Kathy

Everyone say hello to Kathy. In this image the lighting is perfect, and you can see that sensitive little smile along Kathy's lips. There is plenty of positive emotion, so let's use it to create an interesting composition.

Luckily there is plenty of contrast here to cut Kathy out without having to resort to the Pen tool. Using the Extract tool (**Filter > Extract**) it is a simple task to highlight around Kathy. First use the highlighter pen to draw around her – be as rough as you like and go over any areas with 'fuzz' (like hair). Once she is completely surrounded, switch to the Fill tool and click somewhere inside her – if you've been thorough with the marker she should turn blue.

Click Preview and give the machine a few seconds to think. Finally, select the Edge Touch Up tool from the left and go around any areas where it appears that the computer has taken away a bit too much of Kathy.

Once you're happy, click OK and the cloth will be removed for you. Using this tool is preferable to the Pen tool because it can automatically pick up finer detail like the hair and doesn't leave us with such an artificial line around the figure.

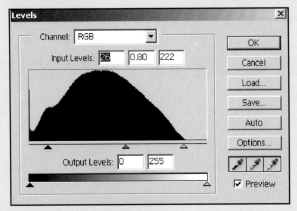

Once Kathy is extracted, it is a simple matter of finding the background to suit her. I've gone for a picture of a bush , as its brightness serves to bring that smile out further – giving her something to smile about, if you like – without there being anything complicated to distract from the model herself. Simply place it behind Kathy's layer, then give it a bit more life with a Levels adjustment layer.

All that remains is to get Kathy to match her sumptuous new background. To my eye, she needs to be looking the other way – no problem; we'll just **Edit > Transform > Flip Horizontal**. All that remains is to use a few copied layers (in my case Screen at 19% then Multiply at 23%) to get Kathy the right color and give her a shadow.

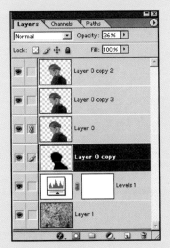

The shadow is created by copying the Kathy layer, then turning the Brightness and Contrast right down on the new layer, before applying a good strong Gaussian Blur. With a bit of transformation, this provides a convincing interaction with the background.

This is a good point to save the PSD file of the work in progress, as the final step is to flatten the layers and apply a touch of film grain using the **Add Noise** filter, set at Gaussian, and with the Monochromatic box checked. And that's it – doesn't she look a lot happier outdoors than she did stuck indoors next to that boring cloth! It looks as if we have captured a real moment in her life. Possibly she just received some good news about a friend, or maybe she's going to Paris in a few days, or maybe she's just a happy person. Who knows, but the composition sure stirs interest.

Of course we need not stop there. We could change the composition by introducing another character and one of my patented gradient adjustment layers. Now something altogether different seems to be going on in the picture opposite, something covert. I don't know about you, but I'd really like to know what's just been whispered into Kathy's ear!

# Face to Face

Given we've just had a glimpse of working with more than one face in the same canvas, let's try another coupling. Here we've got some interesting snaps of Sunny and Ben, who both look a little somber at the moment, perhaps something to do with the lighting.

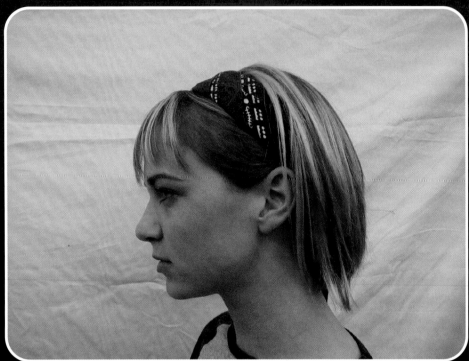

They're easily cut out with the Extract tool and placed together on the same image, using the same techniques as before, including the blur shadow that makes the difference between reality and fraud.

Once we're happy with their position – more face from face than face to face at the moment – we can merge the layers (though obviously keeping a PSD with separate layers might be handy later). In other circumstances it might have been necessary to make color adjustments first, but here the tones seem near identical already.

The Eraser comes in handy here if any of his shadow appears anywhere other than on her (for example in the gap between their heads). OK, we're not quite working in the real world with this image because we're keeping her slightly too close to our 'camera' to be believable, but it all helps the illusion.

The next step is to find a background that'll add something to the message of the picture. The image I selected – the car park at the back of a fairly nondescript building – can play as much or as little a part in the story as the viewer likes. It could be allegorical – the flowers perhaps the ray of hope in an otherwise bleak situation. We can bring that out a little more by removing the blue feel from the image by applying a Color Balance adjustment layer to bring out the more cheerful shades.

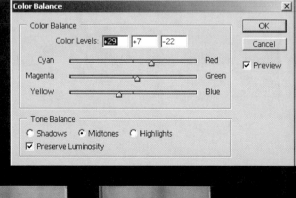

But, as already noted, this image is working on a different level to true reality – otherwise Sunny's shoulder would be wedged into poor Ben's back. So let's play on that effect a little more, by blurring our new background beyond recognition, which gives the image a strong filmic feel. A quick wash over Sunny's face with a the Blur tool (big brush, 50% pressure) completes the effect – somehow our two stars now look to be on the streets of a European capital, with sunlight

A touch of film grain completes the hyperreal feeling of intense French documentary film-making, but for the most part the whole effect is created by the strong Gaussian Blur on the background. In fact depth of field can have a powerful effect on all sorts of dramatic imagery, as we'll see below.

# Depth and drama

One aspect that really throws a picture's context is its composition. You might think that it would be pretty difficult to compose a face with any great effect, but if so, you can think again! Cartoonist Gary Larson (creator of *The Far Side*) said that an early lesson he learned in creating one-panel cartoons was how to employ **depth**. It's a terrific skill to learn when you're getting into creating economic images.

The following image is an homage to the tight visual composers – Larson, and Ingmar Bergman in cinema.

Here's the science part: I lassoed the middleground guy and dragged him onto the picture of the woman in the white top. Then I lassoed the foreground woman and dragged her on top of all that. So we have three layers. Then I blurred the background woman with a Gaussian Blur of 5. Then I blurred the middle guy with a Gaussian Blur of 2. That was essentially it, save a couple of minor extras I'll talk about shortly.

By simply lassoing figures from other pictures I've managed to create a scene of some tension. It could be straight out of a Bergman film. Obviously the woman in the foreground – let's call her Maggie – has been cheated on by Phil and Suzy in the middleground and background. Read Phil's face! The swine! He looks pretty happy with himself. Maggie is *so* aware of the people behind her. Is she looking over her shoulder? Seems like it to me.

The whole thing is composed by the faces – it all fits so beautifully. Big, medium, small; near, middle, far; sharp, soft, blurred.

The other minor things I did to the picture just tweaked that tension a little. In an RGB mode on the foreground layer I added that most cheesy of filters, the Lighting Effect. I used a Default Spotlight, shining up, and I toyed with the levels until just the woman's peripheries were in silhouette.

What does this do? Well, it creates an external element. After all, if we haven't got room in our composition to show an item, we always have room to show how it affects things. So, if we're going for the literal, this could be a candle in front of Maggie – a classic symbol of burning passion. Alternatively, if we dispense with the literal, it could be her fiery and secretive rage against the philandering Phil. She looks a bit mad. The fact that the candle only lights Maggie, leaving the others in regular daylight means this whole thing is a secret between her and us.

Also, the crop of the picture cuts Maggie's face directly in half. She is not showing us her whole face – literally and metaphorically.

The final detail was to put the whole thing into grayscale. This lends that edgy gritty Bergmanesque quality. Life's just like that when you're jilted.

So you can see how the context of an image changes subtly when you start playing images off one another. Have a look at these images, and see how they subtly alter! This demonstrates how crucial context can be to the overall feeling.

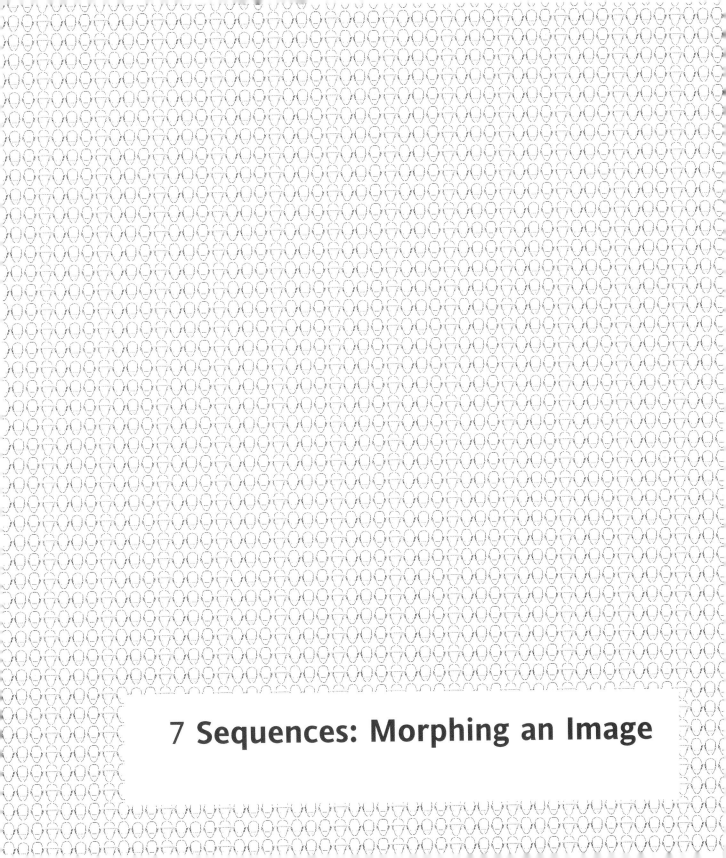

# 7 Sequences: Morphing an Image

In Chapter 2 we looked at the elements of a face that make it strange or unusual. We'll go one step further in this chapter, changing a perfectly ordinary facial feature into an extraordinary one. We'll concentrate on eyes; surely the most expressive feature of anyone's face.

While the dilation or constriction of the eye's pupil is usually associated with change in light intensity, studies have revealed this can also be attributed to emotional changes, which we pick up on, even at an unconscious level. So, information about a person can be conveyed at a glance. This may in part help to explain why we tend to find affinity towards animals with similar shape and size eyes: we look to the eyes to see what is most human.

It's a fair assumption that many of us tend to find more affinity with a dog or a cat than say, a reptile. Perhaps this is something to do with the configuration of a reptile's eyes – to us, their baleful slit, set inside a green or yellow iris is menacing and almost alien-like.

In this chapter we're going to explore this theme using a picture of a human eye, and change it into the eye of a reptile using a sequence of images illustrating the most important changes that will take place in the metamorphosis from human to reptile. We'll then use the sequence of images to create an animated GIF.

Obviously, this type of effect in a movie would likely consist of several thousand frames, but the creation of such a sequence would be based around frames where important changes occur, known as **keyframes**. You can have many other frames in between the keyframes, depending on how subtle or seamless you want your metamorphosis to look.

Before we start manipulating anything, we need to decide **how** we are going to manipulate the action. How do we want the special effect we are about to create to actually work? It's a good idea to plan this out on a storyboard so that you have a clear defined set of goals for the component images you want to create, as well as an understanding of how the different elements will be interacting in order to heighten the realism involved.

To illustrate this point further, let's take a look at the raw material we're going to use.

Our first image is a close up of a human eye, which is taken from this image.

The model is wearing a light base of makeup, but nothing more. If you look carefully, you can see me clutching my camera in the reflection, trying to get as close as possible, and yes, I should have used a tripod.

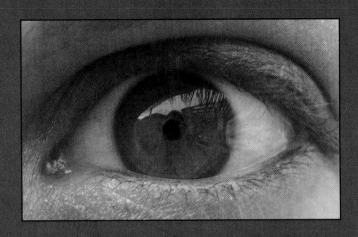

There's nothing particularly extraordinary about this shot. It will serve as our starting point for the sequence and we'll call it Keyframe 1. We are going to create 12 keyframes for this project, with Keyframe 12 being our reptilian shot. Most of the raw material for the final reptilian makeover will come from the following:

I created this image using elements from a crocodile, my cat and a snake; the combination of which I think you'll agree is fairly alien. The final shot will draw heavily from this shot, except it will have some of the added lighting effects which I created along the way. Before we move on, here's a brief description of the tasks I had to achieve to create a suitable image.

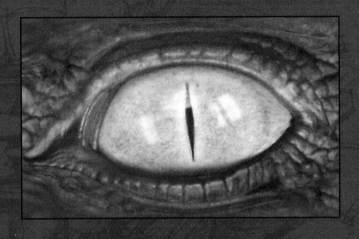

I used a cat's eye as the basis to achieve a realistic looking reptilian eye. Although cat's eyes are not particularly reptilian, they do have a slit, which seen out of context of their fur and once embedded within scales, manages to do a good job. They were also slightly more favorable to me as I have a cat slouching around the house; pet crocodiles are very rarely seen in my study.

In order to construct a believable eye, I analyzed a small picture of a crocodile. The shape and slight color difference were the only important modifications I needed to make. To make the eye look more believable I decided to add reflective highlights by drawing the light spot on the left and cribbed from the human eye picture using a screen (on the right). I was also lucky enough to get some reflection from the cat.

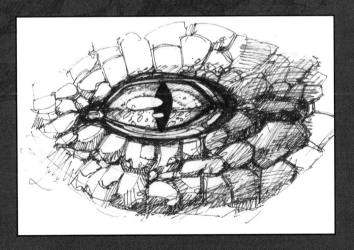

More important than the eye were the scales. First, I enlarged then partly redrew them from my tiny crocodile photo. To achieve this I relied heavily on the Clone Stamp and Healing Brush tools. The color of the original was also a dirty brown, which I changed using a Hue/Saturation adjustment layer. I achieved the rich color by duplicating the layer and then overlaying it on the original.

I simply used the snake as a guideline for the basic shape of the eye socket.

With the raw material complete, I needed to carefully plan out the morphing sequence. I studied my beginning and end keyframes, deciding on what keyframes to make and how they should advance the image from its start to end. The voyage from the start to end state in a believable fashion is dependent on the cohesiveness of your keyframes – don't try to do too much from one to the next. It may sometimes be necessary to go back and insert a whole slew of new keyframes to ensure for a smooth transition.

A final consideration is overe what kind of motion the keyframes will establish. In our example, the metamorphic change sweeps from the eyes outwards, but this could just have easily been the other way around. When you're constructing each keyframe, this macroscopic action is very important if the keyframes are going to hang together properly. Each keyframe must not just advance the change, but it should also keep the style of change constant.

Let's now think about the storyboard for the sequence and establish a brief description for each keyframe.

### The 12 keyframe storyboard sequence

We'll briefly consider some base requirements for each keyframe before actually making a start on manipulating our images. It is important to remember that every image we create must be seen in the context of the project as a whole:

- **Keyframe 1** is the normal human eye without any modification.

- **Keyframe 2** contains an iris enlarged to twice its normal size.

- **Keyframe 3** contains an iris that completely fills the eye socket so we have an entirely single color eye with a tiny pupil in the middle.

- **Keyframes 4 and 5** involve recoloring the iris to resemble a reptile's. This is achieved through fading in a new layer: keyframe 4 will show the new layer at 50% opacity and keyframe 5 will be 100%.

- **Keyframes 6 and 7** involve reshaping the pupil to resemble a reptile's. keyframe 6 will contain a stretched version of the existing pupil and keyframe 7 will introduce the reptile one.

- **Keyframes 8 and 9** involve manipulating the skin color to convey the impression of a continuing metamorphosis.

- **Keyframes 10 and 11** involve manipulating the skin texture around the eye to achieve more reptilian looking skin.

- **Keyframe 12** is the complete culmination of the transformation.

Let's get to work on the basis of the requirements set out above.

## Enlarging the iris for keyframe 2

To begin the project, I used the human eye and reptile eye on two separate layers of the same file – to help get the positioning right. Our first task is to create a mask around the area we want to alter, which is easily accomplished using the Pen tool to create a work path.

Now highlight the iris and copy the area to a new layer. We can do this quickly and easily by using the Elliptical Marquee tool and then scaling it so that it fits perfectly.

If you now use CTRL/CMD-SHIFT-ALT and left click on the work path in the Paths palette, we can create a selection that is the intersection between our elliptical marquee and the path we have created. In this way, we cut off the bottom of the selection where the iris is hidden by the bottom eyelid.

Copy and paste places this selection on a new layer (CTRL/CMD-J). Now let's increase the size of our new layer by scaling it to 120%, maintaining the aspect ratio. Obviously the top and bottom of our new sized layer extends beyond the boundaries of the eyelids (the selection is round, or at least oval, the eye is not), so we need to crop this again by selecting the work path as our guide.

For a little bit of realism, use a 20% opacity eraser (soft edged brush) on the top and bottom of the expanded iris so that the boundary between it and the eyelid is less severe.

In reality (though perhaps reality isn't quite the right word here) we're breaking the illusion slightly. We're expanding the reflection on the eye along with the iris itself, which is inaccurate – the reflection should remain the same size. It's unlikely that this will be picked up as the action is happening fairly quickly at this point, so we'll overlook it.

Already there is something unsettlingly wrong with this person, but let's start to get really bizarre and cover the entire eye with the iris.

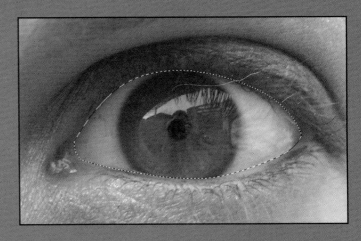

## Completing the iris for keyframe 3

In order to achieve this we are going to make use of the Clone Stamp and Healing Brush tools. Another way to do this might be to use the Liquify filter and distort the edge of the eye until it covers all the area as defined by the work path, although this won't look particularly realistic.

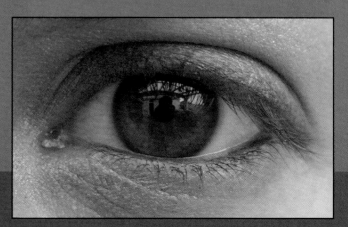

This is quite a challenging task as there's a lot of reflection off the eye, so the area that we can clone will be fairly small. I took quite a few pictures of this eye. This is worthwhile because even if you select one picture to be your raw material, you'll often find that some of the less acceptable shots have some elements of them that are useful.

This is one of those situations – the raw shot didn't have the eye open enough like I wanted it, so I used one of the less acceptable shots with less reflection off the eye, enabling me to record more of the iris.

Here we can borrow lots of iris to use as raw material to fill up our iris layer. I tried to leave a fair amount of the reflection in the eye to maintain that level of realism. What helped was rotating the picture above and using the Clone Stamp and Healing Brush tools to fill the remaining white area in this way.

Two other techniques helped to create realism. I first added an inner shadow – with the loss of the white area, the visual plane flattened rather sharply, and I still wanted the feeling that the eye was recessed behind the eyelashes – many of which I deleted in preparation for the change in the skin.

The one problem of patching together this entire area is that it doesn't come across as smooth – different parts of the eye are of different color and light intensity – I needed something to make this hang together and achieve a level of homogeneity. To achieve this I used a brush of about 5 pixels in width and drew lines out from the pupil to the extents of the eye – in pinwheel fashion. The color of these lines was alternately brown and black – the two main colors in the eye.

After completing this task I applied a Zoom method Radial Blur to the layer about 3 times at maximum strength, which gave me the effect shown here:

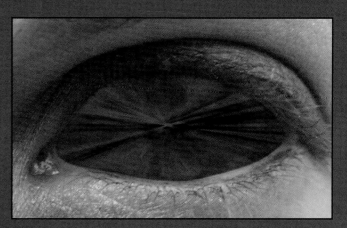

Once I'd used a Color Dodge blending mode for the layer, I found uniform areas of light and dark appearing, using the radial type pattern we find in the muscles of the eye.

Even though we're clearly doing something fantastical here, it's still important to try and ground your ideas in something comprehensible – like matching the patterns of the eye muscles – this just makes the illusion that much more believable. People respond better to stimuli they understand – and can identify with – even if they don't understand where this identification is coming from. For instance, in our example of people responding more positively to other people with dilated pupils, they might not understand *why* they are responding differently, but they do anyway.

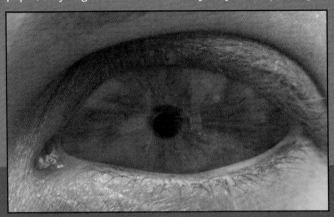

Additionally, I thought we were losing the pupil in such a large iris, so I made it a bit darker by simply adding a layer above it with a black blob and then overlaying the layer. Once again, the boundaries of the layer and the eye were too obvious, so I used a soft edged brush just to blur them a little – great tool, the Blur tool. This blended version works a lot better in my mind.

So the look we have generated thus far, is familiar, but clearly unsettling.

## Recoloring the iris for keyframes 4 and 5

We now need to create a reptile colored eye that is the same shape and size as our human one. We'll Clone Stamp from the reptile eye into the work path shape, creating a reptile eye in the same shape as the human one – not a vast undertaking as their isn't a great deal of difference between the two eyes.

To make the task easier, I duplicated the reptile eye layer and then cut out the reptile eye so that it could float above its human counterpart, enabling me to more easily see what was left to fill. Using the work path, I then created the layer using the Clone Stamp and Healing Brush tools, applying the same techniques of blurring the edges and adding an Inner Shadow layer style.

I didn't find the enhancements I made on the layer to be sufficient, so I went around the edge again with a fairly large soft edged brush using a dark brown, and then applied a Hard Light blending mode on the layer.

Still not enough. I applied another similar layer, this time using a much larger black brush to create a shadow on the eye, because I wasn't convinced that the reptile layer was believable. I wanted the top eyelid to create a shadow on the new eye to make it look like it belonged there. I used a Luminosity blending mode for this layer, to keep the color consistent and so that it wouldn't just appear as a black smudge.

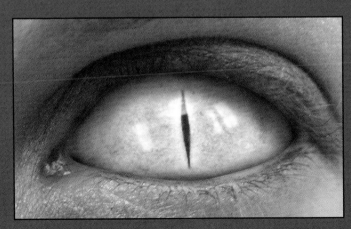

Here another problem emerged: I'd been using my work path faithfully, but now I had this fairly dark shadow from my luminosity blended layer ending in bright pink skin at the edge of the eye, which looked totally fake. Another layer: this time using a fairly small, low opacity (11%), soft edged brush, I went over the area where these two boundaries met a few times to darken them and thus blend them together:

Now, remember, we still need the human pupil. I liked the white area around the black pupil slit though, so kept this in mind when I cut and pasted the human pupil to the layer above this one, then clone stamped the rest of the slit out of the way.

At this point I could have left the keyframe as it was. There was a lot bothering me about the image however. This is one of those projects that, if you are feeling picky, you can look at for hours and every few minutes find a new fault with it.

## Regaining Realism

Technically, the change was complete. But the illusion of reality still needed some work. This is an important part of the project: alter the image the way you want it, then go back and make sure that it's within keeping of the flow of the keyframes *and* upholds the illusion in its own right.

Take a look at the previous picture, while I highlight some of my distress. First, in the original reptile picture, there is shading along the bottom of the eye, as I had clearly recreated here. This is not (and should not) be present in the human eye, though – simply because the eyelash sill of a human eye is fairly thin and will therefore not cast such a dark shadow. This might seem like a minor point, but for me it ruined a lot of the illusion.

The second big problem for me was where the eye meets the bottom eyelid – normally in an eye there is a little bit of liquid here – which gives this area a shiny appearance. I'd lost that by pasting over it somewhere along the way.

There was also a problem with the realism of the human eye pupil, so I added a few layers to help increase the reflectivity of this area so that it looked like a part of the same glossy pale yellow eye and not just some dark spot blobbed on top. This was a fairly simple matter of overlaying diffuse white shapes – kind of like the ones already present on the reptile eye.

My other major concern was that we'd got too far removed from the human eye too quickly – no points of reference other than the pupil remained. Due to this, I added in a similar radial blurred image (as previously described) on top in order to simulate the underlying muscle structure of the eye. Once again I used a Hard Light blending mode to embed the layer into the design seamlessly.

After touching up the bottom of the eye with a thin light line to simulate the moisture, I applied a Blur on this layer and an Overlay blending mode. The blur hopefully took care of the fact that this moisture exists on the eye and the eyelid – it joins them together and exists in the space where they meet.

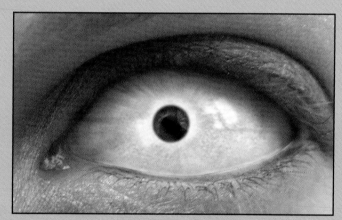

It's often particularly useful to study the natural objects you base your creations on for something to look realistic. Even if it's a completely unreal object, it must be grounded in certain 'observable truths' – visual cues that the viewer will identify with and will therefore tacitly go along with the illusion.

Even now, there are changes I'd like to make to this image, but there comes a point where you must realize that the image will not be scrutinized – it is part of a sequence and will be fairly rapidly presented to the viewer.

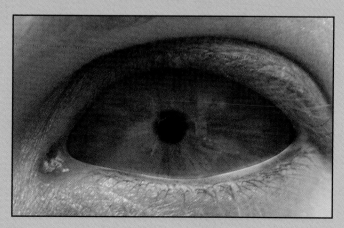

I've pretty much opened up a can of worms now: going back and looking at some of the previous slides I noticed the same problems with the lighting and shading – not as realistic as I'd have liked it to be. It's important to maintain consistency in a project like this, so I went back and retouched our original total iris picture, adding in some of the elements I'd just included.

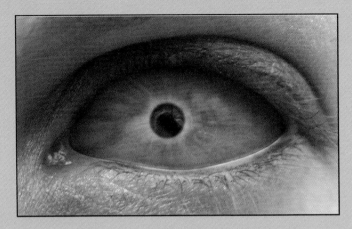

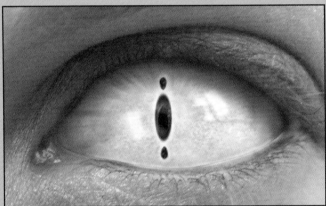

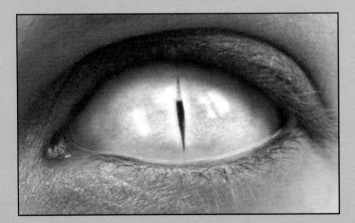

Time to move on – all that's left to do in this part of the keyframe sequence is construct a slide that is half way between the picture above, and our new reptile eye. This simply involved changing the opacity of our new reptile layer in order to let some of the above image show through. To achieve this, I changed its blending mode to Soft Light. It helps to give the impression that whatever is happening to the person, it's starting with the eyes, and it is the eye muscles that are feeling the underlying physical change first.

To add a little bit of flare to this, I left in the new radial muscle layer that I'd drawn and beefed up its color a little bit.

To get this right, I used the Hard Light blending mode for the radial muscle layer which brought a lot of red out of the brown total iris layer below – but only in the areas that intersected with the radial muscle area. In fact, it brought the color out a little too much, so I dropped the opacity of the layer to 57%.

We're almost there as far as altering the actual eye is concerned and we'll now concentrate on applying reptilian characteristics to the pupil.

### Reshaping the pupil for keyframes 6 and 7

Have a close look at the slit reptile pupil and you'll notice that at the top and bottom the line gets slightly wider again. We'll use this feature as the basis for reshaping the pupil by creating two tear drops and morphing them, along with the round pupil into the slit – like water or ink running together to form one complete shape.

Something quite different is now lurking below the surface. To manipulate the pupil, I first duplicated the layer and then simply squashed it horizontally and stretched it vertically a little.

The true reptilian eye is finally revealed in keyframe 7. Notice how this eye is quite different from the one I had earlier, as it is now includes all the modifications I made during my work on keyframe 4. No extra work was needed here; I merely turned off all the other layers that I added for keyframe 6.

## Adding skin color and texture for keyframes 8 to 11

We first need to apply a green bruising to the skin around the eye and remove the eyelashes. The green bruising will spread out from the eye as it engulfs more skin. We are going to use a kind of viral movement to the spreading – like a creeper going up a wall. The next four keyframes (8 through 11) all work together – We see the spread of the bruise and following closely on its heels; the change in the texture of the skin. Because of this, I developed all four frames at the same time.

Keyframes 10 and 11 here are similar to the previous two in that the expansion of reptilian features will move outwards from the eye. In this part of the action there are two different things happening:

- The skin is taking on a reptilian hue, and turning a livid green.

- The scales are beginning to peek through.

The two processes will not occur separately, but almost simultaneously: as the skin turns green, the scales will start pushing through right behind it on the new green skin. So, keyframe 10 will include the start of the green bruising, while keyframe 11 will include a continuation of this bruising along with the start of the scales' appearance.

Another important process taking place at this point is the changing of the eye muscles from human to reptilian. If you look at the final state of the reptile transformation, you'll notice the muscles in the quick of the eye are very different. So, not only are we progressing outwards with these two keyframes, but inwards also.

I started off this sequence by drawing the entire bruising process. Once complete, I was able to work backwards and mask it all away, and then for the purposes of the animation, all I would have to do is grow the mask outwards, giving the impression that the bruise was spreading. Creating this state is one of the hardest parts of the project – let's go through some of the thinking behind it.

We are changing the color of the skin in this phase, but to achieve the level of realism that we want, we need to think about what we are doing to the skin and what's happening to it. The scenario I came up with was one where the skin had a wet, sticky, basic rawness. It's almost like the top layer of skin is dissolving while a sensitive sticky substance emerges. It's the first phase of a new layer that will quickly form scales as it encounters oxygen (in order to protect itself).

Next, consider what this type of skin looks like, and more importantly – what are its chromatic properties? In my mind it was shiny. Let's forget the color of the skin for the meantime, and concentrate on making it shiny. In order to do this, I looked to the original human eye layer. To get started I duplicated this layer. I wanted to draw out the highlights in the skin and in order to achieve this I had the option of choosing between Hard Light, Vivid Light and Linear Light (new to Photoshop 7) blending modes. These draw out the highlights very nicely. Vivid Light is particularly good at this.

 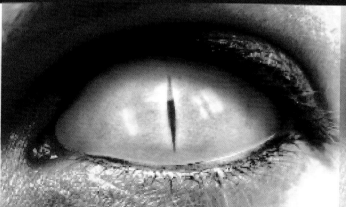 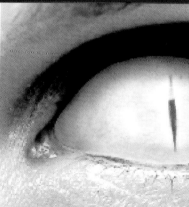

Not bad – I cut the eye area out of this by selecting this area then filling it with black on the layer mask. This certainly wasn't my ending point, though – I knew I'd be using this layer to simply bring out the highlights, and to combine with the final reptile layer. To make a better decision, I decided to start getting the color right. To do this I made a solid color adjustment layer in a light gray-green, dropped the opacity of the layer to around 55% and used a Hue blending mode on the layer.

I wasn't wild about the result. The Vivid Light blending mode was just making things that little bit too vivid (imagine the above image in green instead of orange)–many reptiles look dark and slimy, so I decided to change the blending mode to something more lurid and dank. To achieve this I used Color Burn as a blending mode.

Now the trick: using the **Edit > Copy Merged** (CTRL/CMD-SHIFT-C) menu option on this newly changed Color Burn blended layer, I then pasted this merge to a *new* layer and changed its blending mode to Luminosity. Note that I only copied the prevalent skin area in this way, not the eye, using the mask on the solid color adjustment layer as reference (I could just have easily used the work path I created earlier).

I did this because I only wanted to affect the skin, and not the eye itself, which I would be working on separately. After doing this I turned off the original Color Burn layer – it had served its purpose – and dragged the solid color layer to just below this merged layer. So we now have a copy of these merged layers sitting above them, and being blended in using *Luminosity*. This helped me to achieve my green looking skin and on top of that, I brought out its highlights using this Luminosity blend (which just changes the tone and not the hue of the blend). Remember I obtained these highlights from color burning the blending mode of a duplicate of the original human skin layer.

Let's go over this part again, as it's an important part of any tonal retouching. My aim here was to bring out the light areas of the skin – in order to make it appear shiny. I achieved this by duplicating the layer and then applying a Color Burn blend on the duplicate layer, thus giving me the shininess that I required.

On top of these two layers I added an adjustment layer of Solid Color that colorized the bottom (original) skin layer and the Color Burn layer affecting it, using the Hue blending mode. So, at this point I was applying a Color Burn to a layer and then colorizing the resulting green. I then copied the merged result of the bottom two layers to a new layer (**Edit > Copy Merged**). I did this because I only needed the interesting tonality that I'd just created and not the color (which if you look at the screenshot of the vivid light merge above you'll see is pretty garish!). I used the Luminosity blending mode on this new layer to simply affect the tone of the image below. I then dragged the solid color adjustment layer to below the merged result and turned off the original color burn layer.

Although swapping the layer order here has no visible change, I always try and put the most recently worked on layers at the top of the layers palette if I can, which sometimes helps me understand how I created something when I come back and look at it in a few months time.

There are many ways that I could have chosen to complete this task, though – whether the green Colorize layer (which I now turned back on) is above or below the Luminosity layer makes no difference: either I affect the tone of a layer that's colorizing the skin layer, or I colorize a layer that's affecting the luminosity of the skin layer. There are obviously lots of other layers in the file at this point, but the previous image just shows you the ones affecting this particular part of the project.

Using layers in this way is really useful. The important thing is to start with a goal in mind – in our case, it was to make the skin shiny. Next, you need to consider how you might achieve your aims. Ok, truth be told – I regularly end up flicking through the different blending modes and picking the best result as opposed to having a preconceived notion as to which will be better. It's fun and interesting to see what results are generated – even though certain blending modes might not suit your current project, seeing the various effects is sure to inspire a few ideas for other work.

The main thing to remember is that we're going to need to use a blending mode that affects the tonality of the image and we'll also need an adjustment layer of some sort that will affect the hue. If you can get that far, your job is essentially done – all that's left is the experimentation to get it right for you!

This worked wonderfully on the light areas, but the dark areas were now too dark. To compensate for this, I added a layer mask (which you can see in the previous image of the Layer palette) and masked out some of the darker areas at the top by painting on the mask with gray – kind of like using a low opacity eraser – which lessened the effect of the adjustment layer in those areas:

 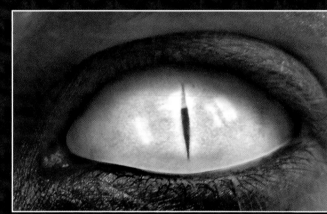

This would then form the basis for the bruising in keyframe 10, but before I could continue, I needed to come up with the final scale application frame.

Because I was adding the bruising and the scales at the same time, I needed both of these (the bruises and the scales) completed before I could complete these skin changing keyframes. To achieve the effect of scales beginning to form, I used the final reptile keyframe and added it as a new layer just above the ones that I'd just been working on, masked out the eye area and used a Soft Light blending mode to melt it into the image

This helped to bring a lot of texture to the skin, particularly the top eyelid. Doing this also took care of many of the eyelashes.

So, upon deciding that these would be my two keyframes, all that remained for this stage of the project was to drop a mask onto each keyframe – which would then be expanded during the animation to portray the spreading of the metamorphosis. Hmm – how do we apply a mask to all those layers?

To achieve this I created a folder and dragged the relevant layers inside it:

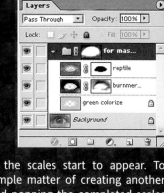

By applying a mask to the folder I could dynamically affect all the layers inside and thus control the effect of the bruising. This then gave me my first keyframe for this section:

As the bruise spreads, the scales start to appear. To achieve this, it was a simple matter of creating another folder above the last and popping the completed scales keyframe inside it. All I needed to do then was adjust the sizes of the masks for the folders and the spread of the metamorphosis was under my control.

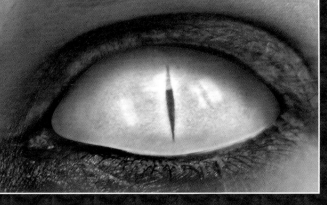 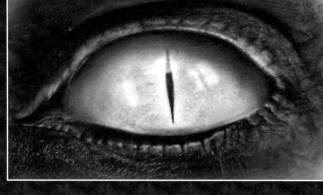

The bruise spreads out away from the eye while the scales follow, as intended. Also notice that although I used my work path to mask out the area containing the eye itself, I've started to remove parts of that mask on the left-hand side to show some of the reptilian eye muscles. As this morphing continues towards the final frame, I basically removed more and more of the mask until the eye on the final reptile slide was not masked at all, and the shape of the eye was changed to accommodate these muscles.

In typical fashion – I love making work for myself – I added in another keyframe. For this keyframe I used the same Soft Light blending mode layer as the basis. I duplicated the layer before changing its blending mode to Hard Light, allowing many more of the scales to show through. I then did exactly the same thing – put this layer in its own folder and controlled the mask of the directory along the same lines.

Perhaps we'd better recap on what's happening here: we now have three keyframes – all of them in folders which have masks attached to them. By manipulating the size of the masks, we're able to control where each one affects the image. So, my plan is:

- The bruise colorize layer mask starts to increase, having the visual effect of the skin around the eye starting to go green and rapidly spreading outwards.

- Once this is underway, I start increasing the Soft Light blending layer's folder mask so that a fairly faint view of scales begin appearing and spreading out in the same way as the bruise.

- Once this is properly underway, I do the same thing with my new Hard Light layer (enlarging the mask size).

In the visual affect, you'll see a bruise spread out from the eye while the skin becomes increasingly scaly. The next picture shows the introduction of this keyframe, with the bruise completely spread, the Soft Light layer half spread and the new Hard Light scale layer just starting – visible to start off with on the tips of the eyelids:

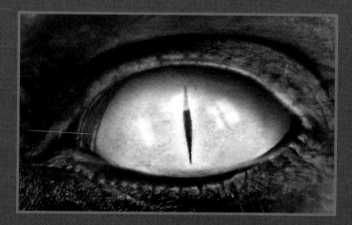

Using this extra frame gave me a smoother transition between the bruising and the scales. Here are the three different states ranging from bruising to prominent scales, which we are spreading outwards with the use of masks:

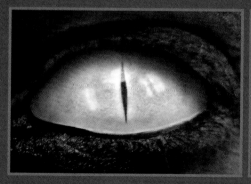

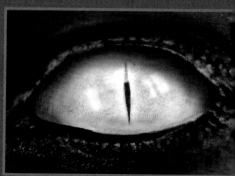

Simple bruise          Soft Light layer          Hard Light layer

This introduction of the reptile eye muscles completed the inner changes that I was talking about earlier. You can see this effect already starting in the picture of the hard light layer above. Also, as I mentioned earlier, as I progressed towards this final frame I made the shadows slightly darker – as the scales jut out more they will cast a slightly darker shadow on the eye, so I tried to be attentive to this change, particularly in the right hand corner of the eye.

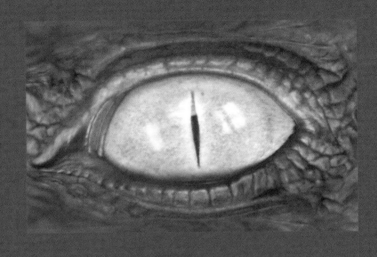

This completes our sequence of keyframes. It's a good idea now to check the consistency of all the keyframes together to see if there are any errors or areas for improvement.

When you're working on each keyframe, they become isolated projects. It's important to drag yourself back to thinking of all of the keyframes as part of one big project. If you wish, you can always add more keyframes to help make your transition sequence look more seamless. That's why I added an extra keyframe when I was developing the skin metamorphosis. Suddenly the scales became totally visible – the transition from the Soft Light blending keyframe to the final keyframe was a little too large. When you're working on a project like this, it's vital to keep drawing yourself back to your main goals; is the animation smooth? Is it believable/credible? Does it maintain the illusion?

With our sequence complete, we now need to set about the task of creating the animation to get from one keyframe to the next:

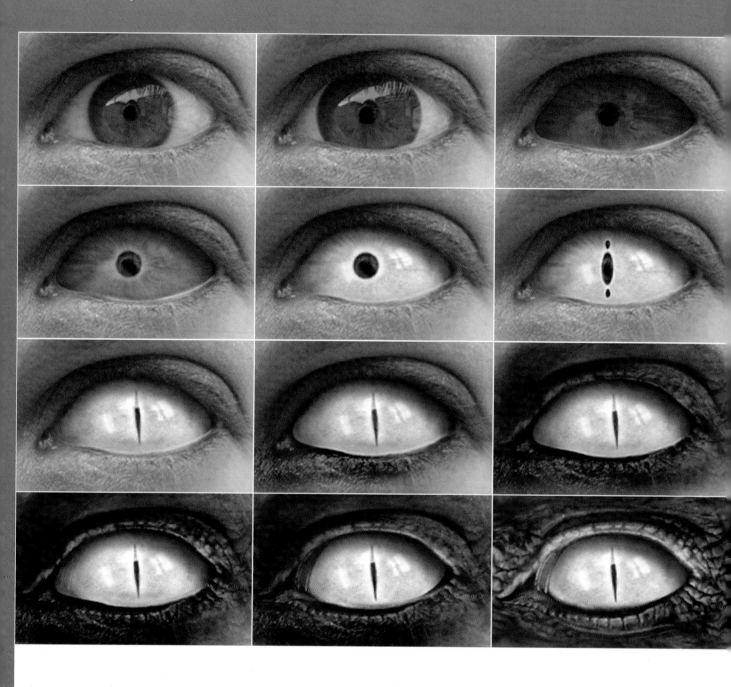

## Putting the sequence together

To create an animated gif using all the keyframes, I used ImageReady's built in animation features. Adobe has created some morphing software but, for our purposes, ImageReady will do fine. Basically, I added each frame separately into the animation palette, starting with frame 1 (the human eye) and ending up with the reptile eye at frame 12. Instead of switching on the appropriate layer from one animation slide to the next, I turned them on sequentially and left them on, building them up from one layer to the next. This meant that when it came to tweening (inserting composite frames between keyframes which are an amalgamation/cross between those frames) I'd have the right opacity.

Let's look at a graphical representation of where I inserted the tweens:

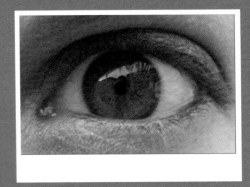

For the first 3 keyframes I didn't insert any tweens because I wanted the action to happen rapidly – it is an explosion of the iris across the eye.

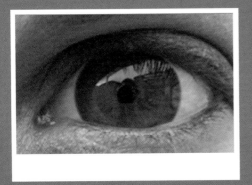 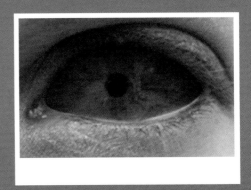

Between keyframes 3 and 4, I inserted five tweens so that the color would fade in nicely.

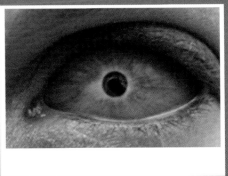

I did the same thing here, inserting five tweening frames between keyframes 5 and 6. This basically meant that from keyframes 3 to 6, a smooth change in color can be evidenced.

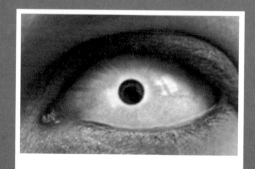

Here again I wanted the action to take place rapidly so left out any tweening frames.

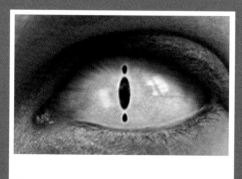

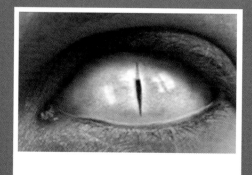

This is where we begin to see the start of the bruising, so I introduced five tween frames between keyframes 7 and 8.

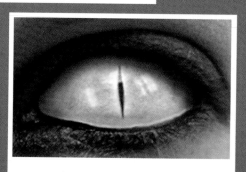

Between each of the next keyframes I also introduced five tweening frames – I deliberately wanted the action here to be fairly slow and creepy – like a fungus.

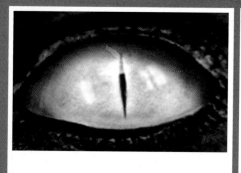

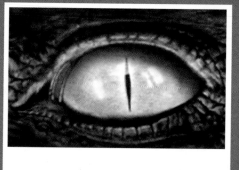

Creating a morphing effect is a time-consuming task that takes a fair amount of mental discipline. It's very important to have a clear idea of what the overall effect might look like at the end and to also make sure that all your frames work towards bringing this effect about.

Even though we created a completely fictitious event with this project, I tried to pay a lot of attention to realistic considerations such as eye shadows and the look and feel of the skin. I focused heavily on anything that would add realism and therefore believability to the finished product. You can download the animated gif (`sequence_primitive7`) from this book's page on the friends of ED web site.

Now that we have the effect, let's see how it might affect the face as the movie zooms out to reveal the reptile:

Not bad – certainly far flung from the original image, and we're safe in the knowledge that we can add as many more frames as we like in order to make the transition as seamless and realistic as we wish.

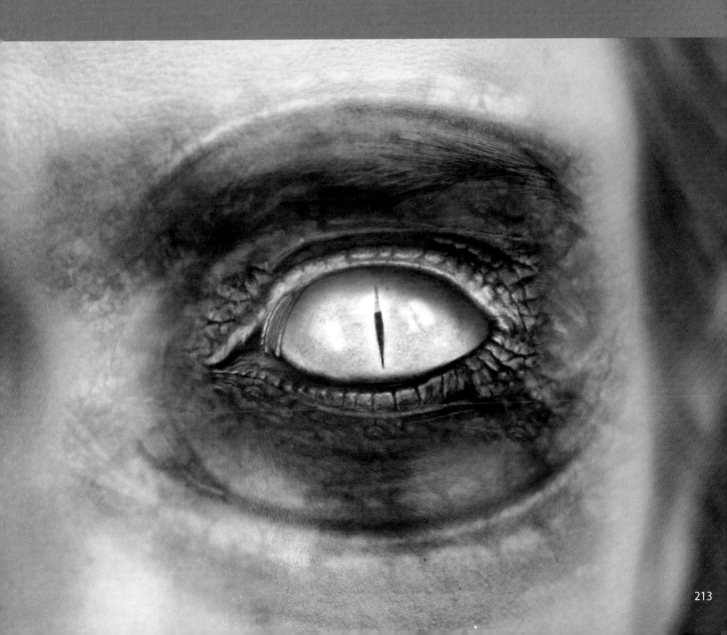

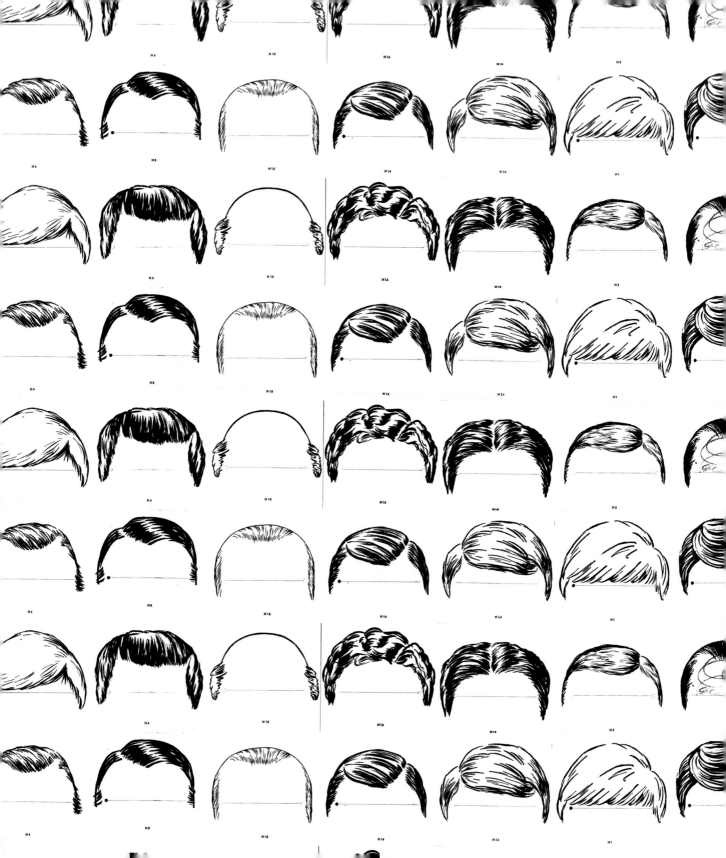

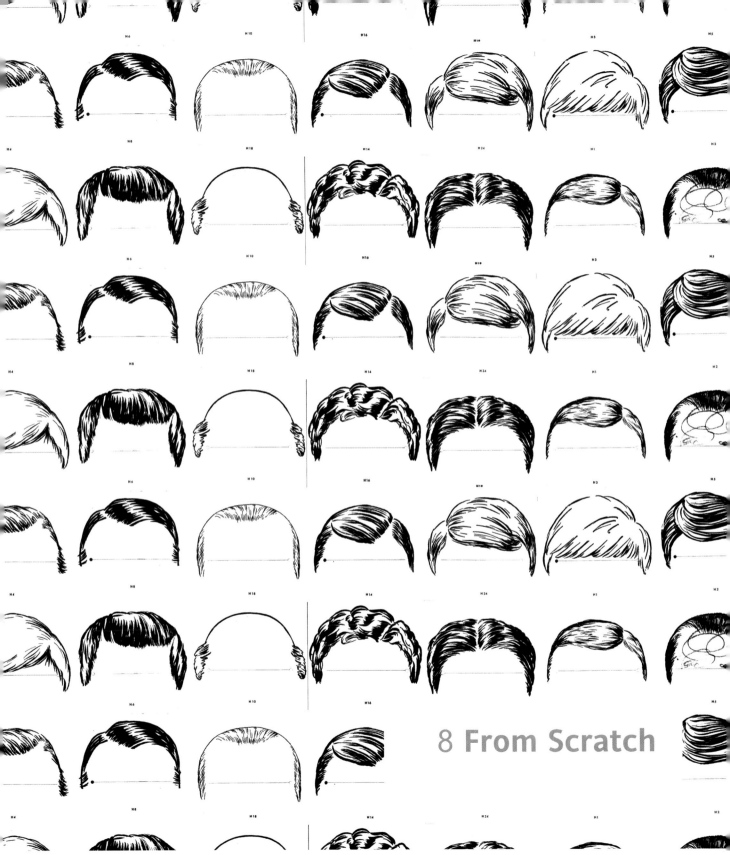

8 From Scratch

I have always been interested in the combination of different styles and techniques in illustration, design, and photography. The common theme in my approach to any form of visual work is to attain one goal: to utilize whichever tool will fulfill the accomplishment of the final image.

This used to be severely compromised by the limitations of construction such as collage and montage and the physical aspects of the construction of the piece: weight and scale. These physical problems all contributed to changing my almost 'Luddite' stance to one of embracing new technology.

As a freelance illustrator/designer/photographer and lecturer, I spend much of my time trying to achieve the best possible output from an idea by utilizing whatever technology is available at the time. The seeds were sewn while attending Art College, where I realized that my style of working required a rethink in order to achieve new and interesting results. It gradually became evident that I needed to become more adept with the computer in order to achieve the ideas that I had in my head.

As my preconceptions of emotionless machines became unfounded, I embarked on an extensive computer learning process – notably, Adobe Photoshop. My aim was to create a harmonious balance between the naturalistic and the technological creative process, and to hopefully find true integration within these areas, more reminiscent of the natural flow of ideas when creating something physical or material.

My main concern then (as now) is that the ideas must be channeled and realized without judgment of the actual processes that brought the work into being, such as drawing, painting, or the computer. These tools only play a part in the production of the work. Essentially, if the work fails, it is the fault of the individual and not the tools employed to produce it.

What is difficult about this chapter, and indeed this book, is justification. Trying to express reasons with a rationale when you're using software with limitless scope for deviation can be difficult. It's important to remember that the infinite joy of 'playing' and discovering those happy accidents, are a pleasing aspect of working within Photoshop, but it's also equally important to remember that these 'accidents' only happen if you know how make them happen.

My response was to create portraits of the 'Four Elements', much in the same mould as those Horoscope 'spot' illustrations found in magazine supplements. I also want to discuss other examples of work in order to illustrate the outcomes of (at times, pure) experimentation.

## Other work

My work tends to have a very rough 'scrappy' look to it, a tarnished, decayed sense of time passing. I have always found dusty old photographs and other old objects infinitely more interesting than brand new items. Collections of objects combined with photographic, painted, or constructed elements all re-occur in most of the pieces you see on these pages.

I am interested in conveying an idea rather than a literal explanation of an image or event – trying to catch that dream-like state, or impression of memory without the coldness of documentation. What I find attractive is the innocence of imagery. When you observe children engrossed in illustrated books, they are absolutely consumed with interest. I like the notion of visual curiosity where the viewer gets involved in exploring the work and creating their own impression of the image, and also seeing something new when the image is revisited at a later date.

I suppose what I am really trying to say, is that I work from feelings and emotions. I really love it when you see a piece of work, be it a photograph, or a movie special effect, and you just think 'What the hell is that? How did they do that?' This is exactly when I really began to realize that I had to get involved with technology and learn the program that would be of most use to me; Photoshop. What I was doing at the time, using construction and collage, were beginning to frustrate me. The final piece never really gelled to the vision I had created in my head, and I felt frequently disappointed by the solid nature of 'real' objects. Just their sheer size, and their lack of transparency led me to getting involved in photography as a means of image manipulation.

I could easily alter the image in the darkroom, but I could precede that with experimenting with exposures and optical effects – this was the fun part. However, I also wanted to combine these images with 'real' objects and to create a fusion of the real, the photographed, and the painted. Enter Photoshop 3.0 (as was).

So, I dived in. At one point, the Photoshop manual and all of those other titles, were my bedtime reading for a number of months, even before I actually owned a computer. Since I knew the theory of how Photoshop operated, I had to try and make a connection with my own style of working, and ultimately making a few mistakes along the way.

I have always been interested in photography and the emotional response to a photograph has always intrigued me. Soon I began to combine photographic objects with natural physical objects along with painted elements. When I eventually got to grips with Photoshop, I began to bring these elements into the application and created work that I couldn't have dreamed of simply by using conventional methods. The malleability of creating new works and new ways of seeing was to become even more potent as time went by. I found new directions where previously I would have spent hours laboring over paint and photo-scrap for it all to end in tears when I realized that the piece never worked, or the varnish wouldn't dry in time for the deadline.

What I found fascinating was the notion of an image's visual 'truth' as the process for image editing became even more faultless and precise. It's really all about the importance of looking. The basic idea is that you are not really sure what you are looking at. Photoshop is used to create the impression of the passing of time: creating something old from a new medium, as if I am trying to hide the use of the computer. I soon relaxed, and took the best from both the natural world and the digital and started to have fun again. Combining the two ways of working created the impossibility of imagery; you are not sure whether it is a painting, a photograph or what. The works in these pages are some of my favorite experiments.

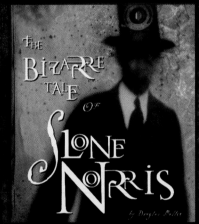

The 'Slone Norris' series of images merit a particular mention at this point. These images were a personal project about the manipulative prerequisite of photography. I based it just before the turn of the last century, in the 1870's, when the new invention of photography led to visual experiments – and fraudulent 'documentary' evidence of fantastical events, such as Sir Arthur Conan Doyle's fairies at the bottom of the garden.

The cover for 'Norris' was a joy to create – one of those rare occasions where everything fell into place in one sitting. There are postal stamp marks, spilt developer fluid, old book spines, grit, coasters, and, my favorite piece, the camera on his hat that was found in a flea market. I sometimes used the scanner to 'capture' 3D objects rather than take several spools of film – it's also a great deal cheaper.

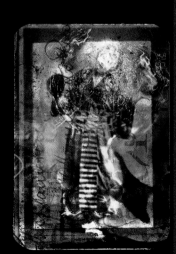

Immediately following the 'Norris' project, I was commissioned to produce several images for an anti-smoking campaign, which (I think) work in a similar mode to the images created for Slone Norris. These images had to be worked out and produced very quickly. Since I had no time to shoot the images to film, I borrowed a friend's digital camera and I was pleased by the outcome. They have a real dirty and scrappy look to them, and this was achieved by layering lots of elements that were burned, torn, and moth-eaten to build up the look you see here.

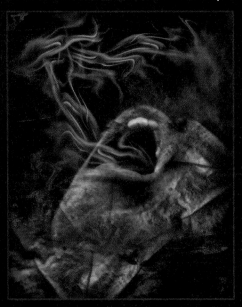 

All of the work in these pages employs similar techniques and approaches, which I will describe later on. Talking about using the scanner as a photographic tool, the next image, 'Ascension' was entirely built up using this technique. On a quiet morning, I decided to play around with concepts and non-linear word play. The scans were manipulated in Photoshop, where I masked out areas to replace them with others, but mainly, the most significant changes were in the colors.

It was fun to see these basic elements composited fairly quickly using the simplest of source imagery (a manikin, a pullover, a cog, a leaf, my hands, and a painting of a sky).

People forget that Photoshop is really two applications in one (if you ignore ImageReady). There is the special effects section – all the filters and fancy tricks generally used by beginners (perhaps a little too much at times) and very occasionally by the rest of us, and then there is the color correction element, which is one of my most frequently used sections of Photoshop. I must confess to only really using a couple of filters. These are: Gaussian Blur, Motion Blur, Unsharp mask and very occasionally, the Wave filter. The rest of the time I use layer masks and the excellent color manipulation tools such as: Color Balance, Levels, Hue and Saturation, and Curves.

When I was given the opportunity to contribute a chapter to this book, I wanted to come up with a series of images that had purpose for each individual image, but also worked together as a set. Since the book was based on faces, I began to brainstorm for ideas. This is usually a painful period where you constantly seek divine inspiration to come up with something that will interest you, but will also be interesting and hopefully, inspirational for the reader. As this book was conceived and designed as an 'inspirations' book on Photoshop, as opposed to a how-to book, I wanted to show what you can achieve with this tool, while also considering the actual design idea.

This was quite daunting for me, as I tend to use Photoshop in a fairly simplistic way. The only thing I really could do was to produce work as if I had set myself, or a client, an actual commission. How can I link images together? The first idea I thought of was to create something in the mould of Horoscope illustrations, where there is ample opportunity to create a surreal set of images that follow a certain criteria and all follow on from each other.

It soon became obvious that a good idea would be to show a set of images, all based on a theme where you could actually relate to the various elements used in the creation of the work. It then became fairly obvious: what about the Four Elements – Earth, Air, Fire, and Water? I knew that I could use found objects, shoot some photographs, combine these with portraits, and still be within the remit of the brief. I also wanted to talk through the creation of these images and discuss the methods I used developing and creating the work.

I began my work in my sketchbook. The first thing I tend to do is make lists of everything that I associate with the particular demand of the job, and generally brainstorm until I get a rough shape of what I may do. How I actually come to do the finished piece is not really a priority at this stage, it's the ideas and visual message you try to think of. Everything else will naturally fall into place later. I try not to be too specific in how the image will turn out as I enjoy the experience of experimenting, but I feel that this must be tempered with a sense of purpose for the image.

So, I create lists of things, and write out dictionary explanations on everything I can think of relating (if only very loosely) to the job. I collect objects, old scans from the many ranks of data CD's I have created over the years – most of them never used, but you can see a few of my favorites in almost every piece I do. I like to assemble work from fragments of other things I have collected in the past. From this initial bout of gathering as much research as I can (and I'll be honest here – I really only use probably around 20% of the stuff I have collected), I then panic, realizing that I have to get the image done. I sketch out about 6-10 versions for each project, and then combine the best sections of each before I either take photographs or start to paint. I intentionally do not spend hours laboring over perfect drawings in my sketchbook. I would much rather get the idea nailed, and spend time on creating the piece. If I was to draw or paint something for the finished image, I would still make short scrappy drawings to get a 'feel' for it, and I would then spend time ensuring any created artwork is cared for in the actual making of it.

So, onto the work...

## Earth

Earth is definitely one of my favorite images of the series. I really knew what I wanted to achieve with this image, right from the start when I came up with the idea of the Four Elements. I knew that with Earth I wanted to have a face submerged in foliage, surrounded with twigs and soil.

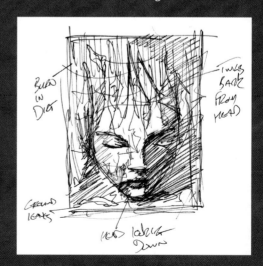

I had shot a number of different facial poses for the right head position, and decided on the one shown here. Since the model is looking downward, it felt perfect for the idea I had visualized early in the development process.

Most of the key features in this particular image are comprised from pictures of debris found under trees and bushes. I wanted to use a fairly limited palette consisting of yellows, browns, and greens to aid the perception of nature and what the Earth is made up of.

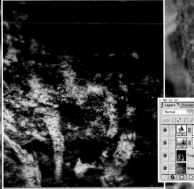

I began by scanning in the face, and toning down the areas that I didn't require in the neck and hair. Next, I combined the scan of moss with the scan of twigs (which I also used in the image of Fire), to give the image a foundation for a background that I could build upon. The colors in these images were not particularly complimentary, so I created a number of adjustment layers (Hue and Saturation, Levels, and Color Balance) to create a uniformity of color tone.

The scan of leaves and dirt was ideal to use as a base foreground. I had intentionally scouted for this shot, as I had a clear idea of what I wanted for the image. This was scaled, and slightly distorted so that it would fit within the image dimensions. It looked slightly odd when it was distorted compared to the original shot, but it just seemed to fit with the image. I duplicated this layer in order to darken the outside border of the image to draw the eye in to the piece, similar to the effect of a vignette.

I then darkened the entire layer using Levels, and created a large 90-pixel feather with the Lasso tool to select the area I wanted to delete. (You can also use a layer mask in order to achieve the same effect – there are always a few different ways to achieve the same effect in Photoshop if you don't follow the conventional wisdom).

The image of the face was then pasted, and laid over the layers described above. I added the scan of stems with an Overlay blending mode so that the image burned through onto the face layer. I wanted to really get a sense of the foliage growing out of the forehead, with other debris in and around the mouth and chin area. The overlay mode didn't really hold enough strength, and was lost in the composition – particularly in the upper portion of the image. I corrected this by duplicating the layer again and applying a layer mask to selectively blend the areas I wanted to preserve in order to achieve a more smooth transition. This was blended by the Lighten mode to fully integrate with the face.

I employed the same technique with the next layer, wanting to give the image some surface grain and to generally add dirt to the image so that it didn't look synthetic and labored. Again, the strength of the image didn't show through as I wanted, so I duplicated the layer and added a layer mask to burn other areas in from the underlying area. This technique worked quite well because each layer had different transparent areas, while each layer also had different blending modes so that different effects could be achieved by the same image.

The image was beginning to take form, and the only thing I really needed to do in order to finish it was to add a couple of highlights in certain areas by blending sections from another image which had the textural qualities I required. I then added a layer filled with 100% black and masked out most of the image so that only a slight border was left. This was then reduced to 40% to 'frame' the image.

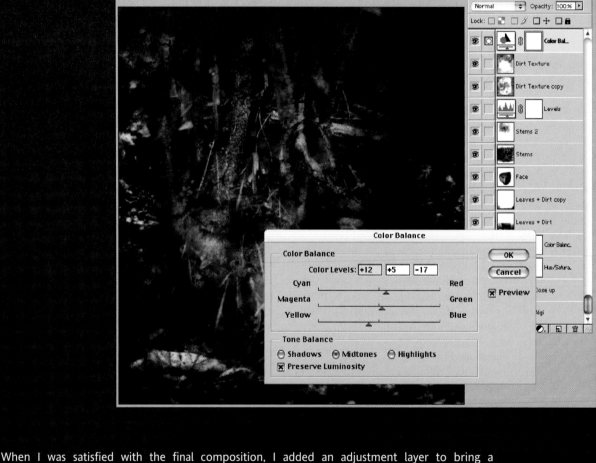

When I was satisfied with the final composition, I added an adjustment layer to bring a uniformity of color tone to the work by tweaking the sliders in the color balance dialog box to bring the image to life.

Since I knew what I wanted to achieve from the very outset, I almost produced this image on autopilot. I think you get to a stage where you are comfortable with the tools and working methods within a program, and you tend to sail through the procedures. The only worry about this is the tendency to relax too much and become lazy with the filters and presets. I think it's always better to find your own path and see where that may lead.

## Air

The image for Air started out life much like most of my images. I immediately thought, how do you illustrate Air? Hmm – the only thing I could think of was smoke, and then I remembered an experiment I did one bored afternoon a few months ago. I took a scan of a flame from a gas cooker, removed the background using the Color Range tool and tweaked the image until it was clean and without any background noise.

I then elongated the image by scaling the height of the flame. To get to the gray image, I de-saturated it and duplicated the layers using combinations of Multiply and Screen to get a wispy, smoky look. I also slightly distorted the selected layer using a gentle Wave filter (from the **Filter > Distort > Wave** menu option) to achieve an impression of movement. You can manipulate an object to achieve an effect much like the trail from a cigarette, by experimenting with the sliders (try around 5 Generators, 10-120 Wavelength, 5-35 Amplitude, with the Repeat Edge Pixels option enabled).

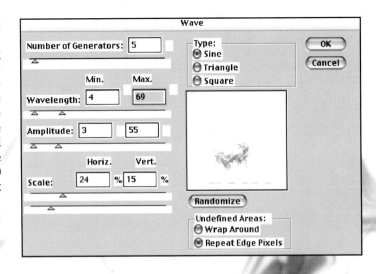

This effect was used to build up the feature of the face you see in Air. Everything you see there is totally created in Photoshop (if you don't count the original photograph, but I'm sure if you persevered you could create that also).

The vapor trails were relatively simple to achieve. Depending on the image resolution, you then set a fairly generous feather using the Lasso tool so that when you delete the area, it gently disappears. (I tend to work for print most of the time, so I always have the image at 300dpi in RGB mode with CMYK preview enabled to help judge roughly how the colors will finally appear. I choose to work in simulated CMYK mode while in RGB because it allows me to have all of the options of RGB without the added file size of working in CMYK – you would have an extra color channel for every layer. While this is not a problem for some, if you are unlucky enough to have a relatively slow machine, this could really slow things down and increase the overall file size of the document). With the selection still active, you can then give a little Gaussian Blur to soften the effect of the trail.

I then copied several versions of the layer, and transformed them in Multiply mode so that the darker areas would blend and the white areas were left unchanged to give the impression of perspective through the smoke haze. This gave the image some depth, and I worked on this technique as the image built up, so that the image remained strong without other underlying layers compromising the effect.

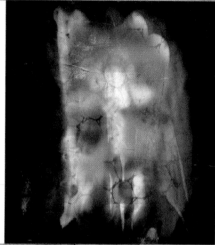

The background was then constructed from a photogram taken from one of my data CD's I mentioned earlier.

I changed the Hue and added a darker background to give some atmosphere. (Photogram refers to a process whereby you expose light sensitive paper by placing objects on top of it in the darkroom. You then take shot exposures from the enlarger at various times, and develop the paper by experimenting with developing bath times. This process means that you can have multiple exposures of different images on the paper without requiring film. It's really a darkroom technique, but the process is very experimental.)

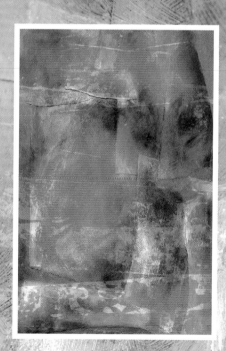

This image is another element that recurs in a lot of my work. Even though I change the colors and the intensity of saturation, it still survives in a lot of other images usually as a background to get the project started. This was created by painted collage, with a few blended elements thrown in to give it some added body. I can't actually remember how I got to this image, but it's mostly a photo-scrap painting overlaid with grit and large scratches using the Overlay and Multiply modes. I tend to experiment with options and stop when it becomes attractive to me. By that time, I have totally forgotten how I got there. This basically stems from painting, where things just seen to happen. That was used for the underlying image for the photogram.

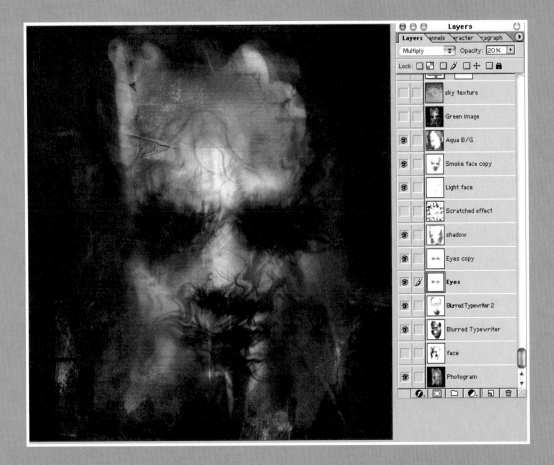

From this stage it's really just a case of following your nose to see what the image requires. To give the image a bit of visual 'realism' and surface grit, I added a scratched texture which I created by taking pieces of adhesive tape and sticking them to a dusty floor, pulling them up quickly so that all of the debris was attached to the tape, and then laying them on clear acetate before scanning them into Photoshop. Next, I deleted the background so that I was left with just the dirt, and then laid this over the entire image.

All of the work you see in this chapter has been blended almost exclusively by layer masks – all in different stages of production. This involves setting the object you wish to 'burn-in' to your image directly over the base layer you want as the main image. Next, paint out all of the image contents and start to selectively paint these back in with relatively low opacities so that you achieve a smoother effect. I generally take breathers between combining more elements, so that I can take stock of what I am trying to achieve.

Without a doubt, the Air image was one of the most difficult to get right, and I am not entirely convinced that it works as a finished piece. I revisited this image around three or four times in the various stages of layering and composting to see if I could improve it. I think the problem is that I find that the first image in a series (I should mention here that Air was the first in this set to be tackled, but I abandoned it and came back to it later) is usually the most invigorating, and also the most disappointing. Air was no different.

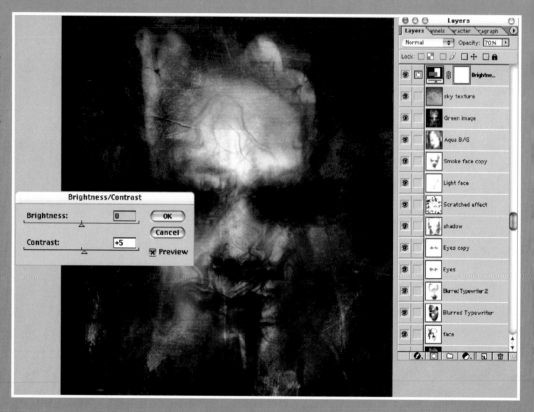

Finally, I created a couple of adjustment layers to tighten up the overall contrast and Levels to create a bit more atmosphere. I flattened the image and converted (a copy) to CMYK format so that I can tweak the channels to get the right intensity of color within each plate. Then the image was put to bed and I could think about the next one.

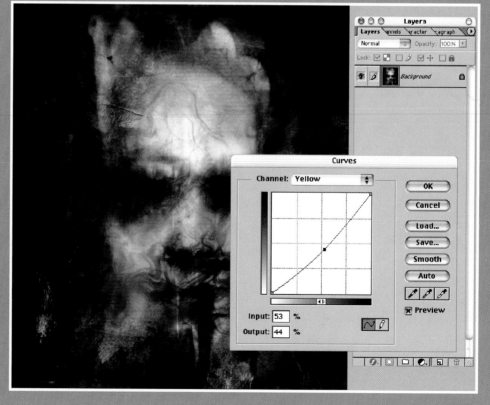

## Fire

The image for Fire began in the usual way with some doodling in my sketchbook. I knew that I wanted to depict a male face with flames for a forehead to try and emulate the intensity of someone, or something, on fire. So, I quickly drew a few ideas and layouts in various forms; some with a torso, some without, some decapitated heads – you get the idea. I just had a fleeting thought of what I wanted to achieve and I wanted it to be almost entirely orange and black, to really make a real contrast of tone and color.

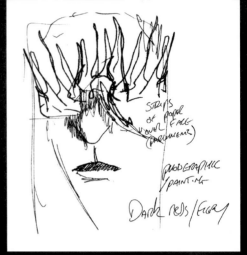

I shot around two or three spools of film as I collected images for this piece. There are quite a few natural elements in there if you look closely; twigs, foliage and some moss growing on a wall that I came across one afternoon while collecting shots for this book.

The twigs were shot in my cupboard at home with a simulated natural daylight bulb and a macro lens. You can probably see the camera shake as I approached clumsily forward towards the object. I don't like to be very technical with photography. I know exactly what I am looking for when I shoot a roll of film because I always sketch out the idea first so that when I collect information or objects, they serve a purpose for the final work. This is the fun stage; getting covered in soil and leaves with the public staring at you blankly as you shuffle through the undergrowth looking for that perfect bit of tree bark. I digress.

Basically, the image of Fire is really made up of these two photographs and a combination of the photographic toning tools in Photoshop. There are also a few bizarre elements thrown in there too, but you would never notice them if I didn't point them out. There is an old piece of parchment paper at the top of the head and some collage text at the foot of the image to help add some visual interest.

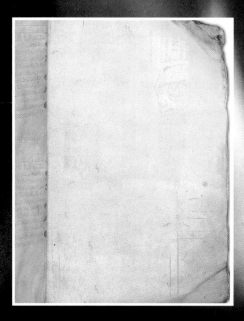 

These elements are almost lost in the final piece, but the image would hold a different meaning if they were absent. The collage of text was a fairly simple image to create; you just start typing letters and words until you reach a happy conclusion. Then you just resize a few of the layers, duplicate some others, invert them to white and subtract them from the underlying layer.

Initially, I toned the image of the face by duplicating the layer and burned out the shirt and part of the neck to give the image some atmosphere with the Soft Light blending mode. This helps to darken or lighten the colors, depending on the blend color – the effect is similar to shining a diffused light on the image. On the layer above, I screened the image and increased the tonal values to help warm the image up and give the impression of a soft glow.

Next, I added the image of moss and created a layer mask in order to burn-in the texture, which added a dream-like quality to the piece. From here, I began to experiment with various blending modes in a bid to disguise the features of the face.

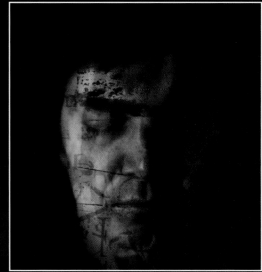

From here, I began to add the scan of twigs and the text collage to give some surface texture. As you can see, the image looks very different without the moss layer, but when you combine them, the image begins to take shape.

As you can see in the middle of the Layers palette, it's here that I added the yellowed parchment on two layers with different blending modes so that each one showed through each other. The first layer was screened at 70%, and the top layer had Hard Light mode at 100%. I turned off the moss layer to show you the difference that layer makes to the overall effect of the image.

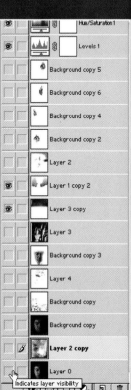

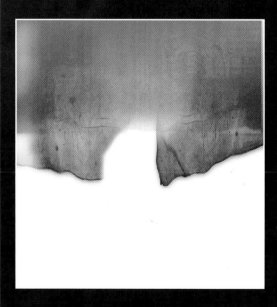

When I turned off the other layers to reveal the parchments, I could see that there are actually three different things going on here; I duplicated the layer, then rotated them in order to mirror each other, then added a slight Wave filter to differentiate them apart. Next, I took another section of the layer and laid it across to top off the image, and created a Soft layer mask to burn out certain areas. I turned the heat up here a bit (please excuse the pun) by tweaking the color balance and increasing the saturation, giving it a warm glow – similar to the treatment described for the face.

When the layers are turned on here, you can see the image beginning to take form. I wanted the top section to be fiercer, so I began adding the scan of the flame to give the image some intensity.

I achieved this effect by photographing a naked flame from a gas cooker, selecting the black from the color range, and deleting it. This is a very useful tool for selecting difficult areas of color – by dragging the slider in the dialog box until you have the required amount of color selected. Of course, you still have to alter the selection by adding or subtracting from the selection when you click OK, as it does tend to pick up other areas that aren't required. I followed the same procedure for the tones of blue until I was left with just the red and yellow of the flame. I softened the edges by running a 3-pixel blur over the image so that there were no hard edges. I then duplicated several versions of the layer, and distorted them so that they appeared as different flames. Again, I used a combination of blending modes (Screen for all the flames here, set to between 70-100%) so that they overlapped, but while striving to maintain the relative color saturation within the tones.

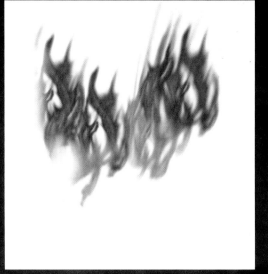

I worked on these separately so that I could create a sense of perspective by blurring the bottom layers and sharpening the overlying ones. There are only four flames here, but there appears to be more. By adding some Motion Blur and Gaussian Blur, you can achieve a fairly realistic effect – much as I did with the smoke in the Air image.

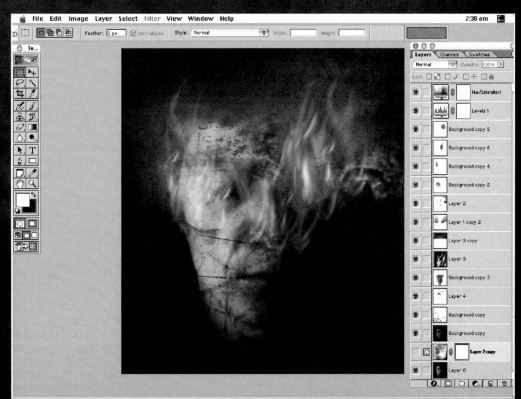

When these elements are combined, you get close to the effect of burning from within the face. I intentionally wanted this image to be fairly simple, and not to add anything extraneous to distract from what I was trying to achieve, which was an almost iconic portrait.

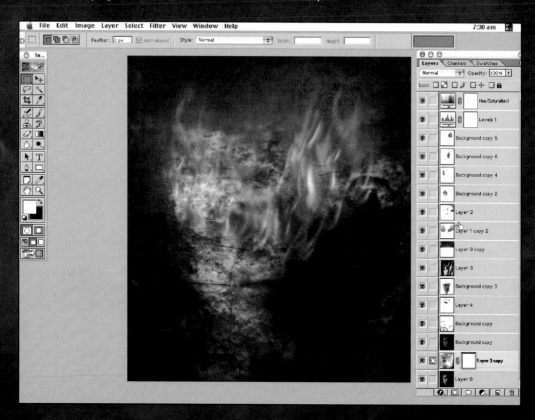

Finally, and as usual – I color corrected the overall tone of the piece. I wanted to lift the whole image tone as I felt that it was rather dark in certain areas. This was achieved by a combination of adjustment layers (Levels and Contrast) so that I could get an overall 'feel' to the almost-completed work. I then brought out the red tones by creating a Hue and Saturation adjustment layer (you could also use the color balance if you wish, as this too achieves a similar effect). Sometimes I look at the layers individually in order to see if there is anything that is not required, or a section that I maybe forgot to mask out. This is fairly typical of me really; I like to work quite messily as I find that this gives the added vibrancy that I like about painting, even though I'm trying to recreate something which obviously has no surface.

I am fairly happy with this one. As it was the second created for the series, I began to settle in to the vibe of what I was trying to achieve.

## Water

I was pleasantly surprised with the way in which Water turned out. I managed to turn this image around fairly quickly by experimenting with the main features of the face that were actually just exposure tests. I liked the way they looked when I got them back from the developers, so I decided to use them.

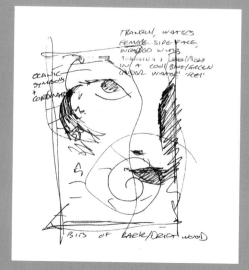

The final image is pretty much exactly the way I planned it, but since I draw ideas without any color reference (I prefer to judge the color as I go along, depending on the 'feel' I get), I was pleased with the quality of luminance in the subtlety of the blues and greens. This is quite a tricky part of the spectrum to get right, as it can easily look very acidic and garish.

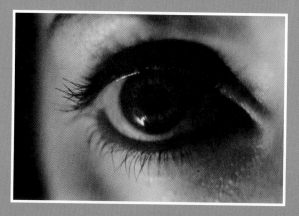

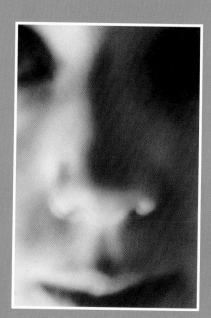

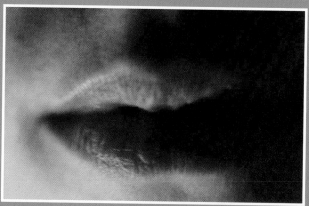

I converted the photographs to black and white after being scanned. I was not really impressed by the original colors anyway, but I tend to desaturate most images and build them up again using combinations of the Color Balance and Hue & Saturation adjustment tools. The images needed a bit of tightening up, so I gave their levels a little nudge and pushed up the contrast a little. I find that converting a color image to grayscale loses quite a lot of image 'bite', and always needs a boost to simulate tones of a real black and white photograph.

The three images of the face, and the images shown above are really all the main elements that make up the image. Again, I have to adjust the colors fairly radically to make them all work within the image. I really wanted to give the impression of the face submerged underwater with reeds and, well, watery things.

The facial elements were collaged together using selections from a scan I had of a grainy texture – this was another of my 'sticky-tape' experiments. I wanted rough borders around each element of the disembodied face to further the sense of dislocation. Eventually they were all toned down to darken some of the lighter areas, and selections were made in some areas to totally blacken the gray areas. When I was satisfied with the result, I merged all of the layers together to conserve disk space and file size, before moving on to the other elements. I realize that when you do this there is no way back, but I like the finality in the point of no return. You make a decision and stick with it. The one thing that I am not a fan of in Photoshop is the History palette. I really prayed for it at the time I thought I needed it, but when it arrived, I was not so sure. There are too many options to go back and constantly change things, and you loose the immediacy of the work. Mistakes in images are what I find interesting, rather than the perfect 'clean' image.

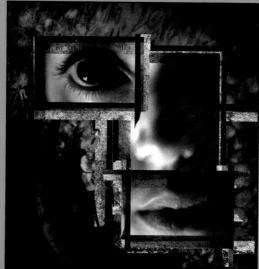

I combined the two images of water and the beach stones using layer masks and a healthy 450-pixel brush painted with various percentages and transparencies to quietly burn areas in and out of the image. This image was slowly manipulated over a couple of hours, and elements sort of 'floated' into the image as it merrily progressed.

When the water and the face were brought together, the image slowly began to take form. Obviously, the face required some color in order to balance and integrate with the background, so this was achieved by overlaying the scan of surface water with a Hard Light blending mode which multiplies or screens the colors depending on the blend color.

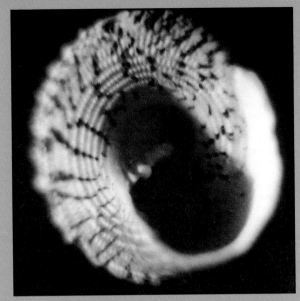

The bottom left of the image required something to fill the empty space. I tried numerous ways of adding seaweed and other beach-combed objects, but I found a small shell that was lying in the bottom of one of my collection boxes seemed right for the image. This was photographed at severe proximity using a macro lens in order to blur the edges and increase the depth of field. I sometimes simulate this effect in Photoshop by drawing a large feathered selection using the Lasso tool, usually about 80-120 pixels inside the area, then inverse the selection and apply a Guassian Blur to the outside edges. Thankfully, this image was perfect and didn't require any forced perspective, although I did colorize it with the same technique as I described earlier.

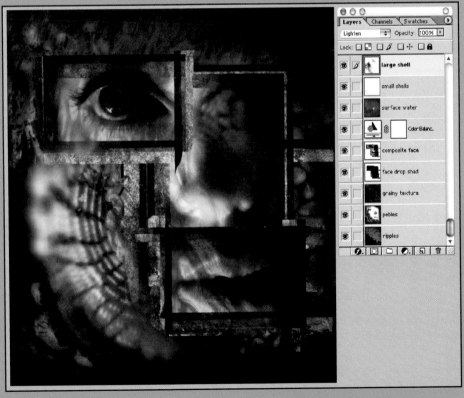

I duplicated the shell layer several times, as I wanted to create more shells down at the bottom left of the image. These were copied, a feathered selection was drawn around each one, inverted, and their levels increased to darken the edges. They were placed behind the larger shell seen in the foreground, and given a soft blur to pull them back.

Finally, I selected the water surface layer, copied it and extracted the highlights by sampling the lightest tones. This was achieved using the **Select > Color Range** menu option, which allows you to increase or decrease the amount of selection within the area using a sliding scale. I then feathered the edges by 3 pixels so that I would not have a hard-edged selection, then inverted and deleted the selected areas I no longer needed.

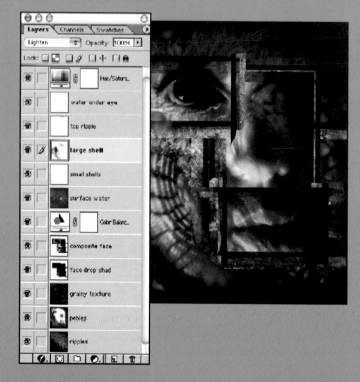

I used parts of this layer to highlight areas under the eye, and at the top of the image used the Screen blending mode, which achieves a similar effect to painting over an area with bleach. My favorite part of this image is the water ripple under the eye. These are additional little details probably lost to the viewer, but I find them important to the overall effect. I think it maintains an interest when the image is revisited. Hopefully when you read these methods, you'll look again at the images described and find something new that you may have missed.

### And in the end...

I hope that you found something of interest in these pieces, or even discovered a way of working within Photoshop that you'd never considered before. We have only touched the surface here, but it's up to you to find your own direction and hopefully find some inspiration in the techniques within these chapters.

This book's focus on portraits shows just how much you can actually produce on a particular theme if you have a purpose behind what you are trying to achieve, rather than using the tools just for the sake of it. However, the actual impulse to do this stems from creative thinking: this is almost (well, for me anyway) an automatic response. It's similar to cooking – you have a clear sense of what you are doing, but you still have to dip your finger into the mix to taste it. Even with the right ingredients, you find that it alters every time depending on your intention. You make informed decisions regarding what you know about composition, light, tone, and color and apply these principles to the function of your particular software. These 'fun accidents' and the notion of 'playing' are terms I use fondly, but not literally. It is informed choice. Therefore, you experiment with what you have at your disposal in line with certain artistic principles and a design methodology.

To explain the nature of creativity is very difficult. Linear rules seldom apply, and while you can research into this area, you unfortunately cannot guarantee you'll get it. It's vital that we do not solely rely on generic methods in our work with Photoshop. I once heard a wonderful quote by the Jazz bass player, Jaco Pastorius, who once replied to a question regarding his very individual and complex style of playing, 'Cleverness is no substitute for true awareness'.

Have fun.

The index is arranged hierarchically, in alphabetical order, with symbols preceding the letter A. Many second-level entries also occur as first-level entries. This is to ensure that users will find the information they require however they choose to search for it.

## DESIGNER TO DESIGNER™

friends of ED writes books for you. Any suggestions, or ideas about
how you want information given in your ideal book will be studied
by our team.Your comments are always valued at friends of ED.

For technical support please contact support@friendsofed.com.

Free phone in USA: 800.873.9769
Fax: 312.893.8001

UK Telephone: 0121.258.8858
Fax: 0121.258.8868

## Photoshop Face to Face – Registration Card

Name ...........................................................................................

Address ........................................................................................

City ...................................................State/Region ....................................

Country ...............................Postcode/Zip .................................

E-mail ..........................................................................................

Profession:  design student ☐  freelance designer ☐
part of an agency ☐  inhouse designer ☐
other (please specify) ...........................................

Age: Under 20 ☐  20-25 ☐  25-30 ☐  30-40 ☐  over 40 ☐

Do you use: mac ☐  pc ☐  both ☐

How did you hear about this book?.......................................................

☐ Book review (name)...................................................

☐ Advertisement (name) .............................................

☐ Recommendation .......................................................

☐ Catalog ..........................................................................

☐ Other ..............................................................................

Where did you buy this book? ...............................................

☐ Bookstore (name) ...............................City...................

☐ Computer Store (name).........................................................

☐ Mail Order..........................................................................

☐ Other..................................................................................

How did you rate the overall content of this book?
Excellent ☐   Good ☐
Average ☐   Poor ☐

What applications/technologies do you intend to learn in the
near future?.................................................................................

.......................................................................................................

What did you find most useful about this book? ...........................

.......................................................................................................

What did you find the least useful about this book? .......................

.......................................................................................................

Please add any additional comments .............................................

What other subjects will you buy a computer book on soon? .........

.......................................................................................................

.......................................................................................................

What is the best computer book you have used this year?

.......................................................................................................

*Note: This information will only be used to keep you updated
about new friends of ED titles and will not be used for any other
purpose or passed to any other third party.*

**DESIGNER TO DESIGNER™**

N.B. If you post the bounce back card below in the UK, please send it to:

friends of ED Ltd.,
30 Lincoln Road, Olton,
Birmingham, B27 6PA. UK.

---